Where to
Find Tomorrow

Where to Find Tomorrow

A Zero-Cost Road to Better Public Schools

Nancy Fairley Ramseur
and
Mary Ramseur Lindsay

REGNERY/GATEWAY, INC.   *South Bend, Indiana*

Dedicated to the memory of our parents

Mary MacMillan and Frederick Henry Ramseur

Their determination to provide an education for
their children, their insistence that each take
advantage of the privilege, and their love and
sacrifices made this work possible.

Contents

Acknowledgments

Where to Find Tomorrow is the result of the genuine concern and willing labor of countless friends, fellow educators, and students. We take this opportunity to introduce and thank them.

The first steps in any endeavor are the most difficult. Miss Doris Kruedener encouraged us to put into writing our experiences and ideas about education. Mr. Richard W. Lloyd of Camden, South Carolina, and Cotuit, Massachusetts, sought the aid of national educational leaders to review and criticize the system. He gave much of his valuable time in reviewing our work, lending a sympathetic ear when needed, and encouraging us to pursue our goal when otherwise we might have faltered.

Developing the system and putting it into practice naturally preceded the writing of this book. Camden teachers and administrators volunteered their help. Mr. Francis A. Snelgrove, former principal of Camden High School, Camden, South Carolina, allowed the system to be implemented in the school The first teachers to venture into the new and untried system and thereby lead others to follow were Mrs. Willie Cox and Miss Ann Wolfe. We are indebted to those who have helped expand the system by using the method in their special fields, by typing, by proofreading, by making suggestions, and by continually encouraging us. Mrs. Becky Milling Brown designed the elementary education program under Ramseur Pilot Light (RPL); Mrs. Rosella Cox and Mrs. Mary Elizabeth Boykin applied it to commercial subjects; Dr. Maurice Cherry, foreign languages; Miss Lee Craig and Mrs. Henrietta Outzs, English and English Composition; Mrs. Mariemma Funderburke and Mr. Thomas Bostick, mathematics; Mr. Leroy Caulder, Mr. Clyde Jones, and Mr. J. C. Goodwin, administration; Mr. Clyde Jones, Mr. J. Coke Goodwin, and Mrs. Vicki Granger, science. Other teachers who aided in expanding RPL within the subject fields were Mrs. Joan Inabinet and Mrs. Jean Pruett in the English program; Mrs. DeSausseur McCutchen and Mrs. Sally Jackson, foreign languages; Mrs. Mary K. Watts and Mrs. Katherine Crider, physical education; Mrs. Andrea Norris and Mr. R. L. Cox, social studies and history program; and Miss Ann Wolfe in the art department.

Others who adopted the system in their subject fields are Mrs. Jean Cave, Miss Emily Bruce, Mrs. Naomi Quillian, Mrs. Rosemary Ayer, Mrs. Frankye Hull, Mrs. Mary Anne Blaskowitz, Mr. Glenn Inabinet, Mr. Thomas McLester, Mrs. Susan Durant, Miss Myrna Gordon, Mrs. Kay Polk, Mrs. Nell Marshall, Mrs Aurelia White, Mrs. Marsha Cashion, Mrs. Sandra Lee, Mrs. Sandra Fitts, Mrs. Glenn Tucker, Mrs. Sherry Patterson, Mr. William D. Chivers, and Mrs. Glenda Crumpler. Mrs. Joanne Geiger, secretary, has for years helped in seeing that every RPL student's record showed that he had participated and that all transcripts carried a letter explaining the system.

Mrs. Margot Rochester, formerly of Camden High School and now of Lugoff-Elgin High School, has given many hours to the support of RPL by teaching English and English composition in the program, participating in conducting a field course on the Ramseur System, and expressing her belief in the merits of the system by her continuous encouragement to the completion of this work. Mrs. Mary Younger Clark has contributed her knowledge and experience in library science, participated in the implementation of the system in Camden High School, served as guest lecturer to classes on RPL, and given her unfailing support to the system from its inception.

When we needed the advice and support of professors of education, a man of reputation, vision, and patience listened because of his natural curiosity, innovativeness, and progressiveness of thought. Dr. John Coan Otts, then dean of the College of Education, University of South Carolina, is this man. An advisory committee comprised of members of the faculty of the College of Education: Dr. Kathryn B. Daniel, Dr. Larry Winecoff, Dr. Joseph Bowles, and the late Dr. Ross M. Coxe, was formed and chaired by Dr. Otts. Dr. Lawrence Giles served as our advisor and Dr. Frances O'Tuel has been a great supporter of the system and to us.

Requests from other schools, the need to protect the system from misuse, and our belief that the program will benefit young people throughout the country led us to decide to write this book. Many tasks that were necessary to completing such an undertaking were shouldered by Mr. Ed O'Cain, Mr. W. F. Nettles, III, Mrs. Mollie D. Nettles, Mrs. Elizabeth W. Marshall, Mrs. McCoy Hill, Mr. John Bonner, Dr. Gaffney Blalock, Mr. and Mrs. Blackburn Wilson, Lt. Col. L. T. Chapman, and Mrs. Kay Polk who gave part of her vacation to type the manuscript.

Editing the material was the final and most important step before publication. Mrs. Ethel Sweet was the first who generously donated her literary talent. We also dared to approach the well-known writer and lecturer, Mr. Fergus Reid Buckley, for his advice. He gave, instead, over a year of his time and talent. Our debt to Reid goes far beyond the preparation of the book; it was he who contacted Regnery/Gateway, our publishers. Our correspondence with Mr. Regnery, Benjamin Barrett and Henry F. Regnery has been most helpful and pleasant.

Henry F. Regnery's visit to Camden to discuss final plans for the book gave us a chance to meet him, an opportunity we shall always cherish. His untimely death in a plane crash May 25, 1979, saddened us, but we are grateful we had the opportunity to meet this delightful, warm, young man.

Families sacrificed the most in their patient waiting for meals that are late and sometimes burned while we decided such serious matters as a comma or no comma. We, therefore, thank Shannon, Sr., Sally, Shannon, Jr., Nelson—husband and children of Mary Lindsay—for their understanding when we were derelict in our duties as a wife and mother and an aunt. We thank you, also, Thomas, Henry, Yogi, Sam, and Willie.

Thousands of students have contributed through participation in and evaluation of the program. We wish it were possible to thank each of them by personal reference; however, we hope they have been aware all along that their future, their tomorrow, is the reason for this effort.

N.F.R.
M.R.L.

*Our special appreciation to Fergus Reid Buckley,
who made* Where To Find Tomorrow *more than a dream
searching for reality. The final form of our book is
due to him.*

Where to Find Tomorrow

Chapter I
An Introduction to the Future

*The alarming decline in education • Attempts to
salvage the public school • A solution from teachers
• Objectives of this solution*

This is a story of the love of parents for their children,
society for its young, the present for the future. It is a
story of humanity's quest for a brighter tomorrow. The
search might well begin in the public school.

With the inception of the dream of popular government, a well-educated citizenry was held to be essential. But the very foundations of our public schooling
have been considerably shaken in the past decade, and
attempts to rebuild and strengthen the structure have
instead further weakened it. The alarming decline in
standardized scores and poor graduate performance
are frightening. Violence in our schools is growing in
inverse proportion to the decline of academic and vocational achievement; students' attitudes reflect their
disillusionment with the educational fare and their
lack of respect for school authorities who fail to control
insubordinate, violent, and even criminal behavior.
The effect on teachers has been devastating, as they
have been required to assume the roles of untrained
and unprotected guards of students who, in cases, become delinquent for lack of perceived direction. And
the taxpayer is unhappy with the proliferation of
government-sponsored programs that devour increasing millions of hard-earned dollars yet show no return

in educational interest on the capital so extravagantly invested.

Supplying American schools with materials, programs, and advice—and not a few nostrums—has become big government business, creating department after department at every federal and state level, entangling our schools in such a jungle of bureaucratic kudzu that you can barely make your way to the belltower. The concern of our government is sincere. The economy is dependent upon the excellence of our public education; the professions—law, medicine, engineering—and the working force of skilled and unskilled labor can hope to be only as good as the primary and secondary educational system that trains the young. It is a truism that today's classroom is the world tomorrow; the student today is tomorrow's adult citizen. But despite the deep commitment of our society to the quality of what the public schools dispense, mistaken advice and huge and complex government programs too frequently cripple the educational mission. The fault, we believe, lies in the flow of directives that issues always from the summit down to the plains where schooling actually takes place, with no feedback from those persons most intimately connected with teaching the young. Those who today dictate school policies know least about education.

For all the clamor, one voice has been silent. The teacher, who best knows the real needs of our schools and the most practical way to meet those needs, and who, moreover, is the one trained to do the job, is seldom heard from. Why? Are teachers apathetic? Are too many demands made upon their time in meetings, crowded schedules, and paper work? Are they silent because they have been overruled whenever they have

raised their voices? Are they not allowed an academic
opinion? Do they fear for their jobs? Do they fear that
speaking out may label them as malcontents or mis-
fits? Is it easier, and sometimes safer, to vent their
anger and resentment in the teachers' lounge among
fellow workers? Are they confused by the avalanche of
new administratively imposed programs that they,
personally, may have had no opportunity to approve?
Whatever the reasons for their silence, they must be
heard, for if an educational system is not viewed by the
teacher as possible and challenging, then students will
not be served regardless of its merits.

We are teachers who want to speak and to be heard.
We are the children of parents who believed that
second in importance to loving their children was impressing upon them the value of education. Our experience spans the last two decades; and it has been with
deepest sorrow that we have seen our schools unneces-
sarily change from symbols of hope for a better future,
which was traditionally opened to the student through
the sometimes hard but so often exciting process of
learning, to institutions of instant credit, designed to
be fun and games all the way, guaranteeing social and
economic elevation to everyone irrespective of his efforts, and allowing—even providing for—the anarchic
and sometimes violent eruption of any and all frustrations. We speak from the classrooms and halls of a
real public school, not from an office, laboratory, or
dream castle. Our theories arose from personal involvement; we have tested them at work, teaching;
and we live with them every day of the school year. We
have taught a variety of courses at grade levels seven
through twelve to students representing a wide range

of intellectual ability and social and economic backgrounds. We are familiar with small schools and large. And through personal contact and research, we are acquainted with educators, systems, and teaching programs throughout the country.

The system we present here realizes two objectives—(1) it "individualizes" education of the young in a practical and true manner; (2) it creates a climate within the school that insures the effectiveness of this instruction. The Ramseur Pilot Light System for custom-tailored teaching was first tested in Camden, South Carolina, in 1964 and has been in practice since that time. The design is simple. It remains constant while procedures may be altered to meet specific needs. This allowance for flexibility does not distort the basic approach. The Ramseur System (or RPL) is not separate from, nor independent of, the total school curriculum. It encompasses the entire curriculum without controlling individuals; i.e., the plan serves, *it does not dictate.*

For its survival, a democratic society is dependent upon both educated leaders and an educated populace. Education therefore must be designed not only to cultivate the mind and inculcate academic and vocational skills but also to develop responsibility to self and to country. This the Ramseur System accomplishes.

In order for all children in a classroom to benefit from the education they get, they must be taught what they need and what they are capable of learning at the propitious time, regardless of age or grade level. They must be made aware of the measure of their achievements. Only then can they recognize what they can contribute to society.

The Goals of the Ramseur System of Education

1. Despite large classes comprising every background on the social and economic scale, to teach all students according to their abilities.

2. To encourage interaction within the classroom.

3. To enhance the student's "self-concept." (This is educational jargon that simply means how students view themselves in their relationships with other students, parents, and teachers.)

4. To stimulate the teacher as well as the student, while allowing both to express their individuality freely.

5. To encourage teachers to work together—which fosters a natural "teaming" (more educational jargon) of their expertise.

6. To create a program of instruction that makes use of the expertise and experience of the teacher yet incorporates the wishes of the child while protecting the child from immature and unwise decisions.

7. To establish a grading system in which the student takes part, through which the student is encouraged and stimulated rather then stereotyped, and through which the child learns to take responsibility for his decisions.

8. To establish an independent study program available to each student according to ability and choice.

9. To emphasize actual learning by restoring reality to grades.

10. To foster integration between races—to equalize educational opportunity realistically so that students, as individuals, rather than as members of any group, may achieve their goals without being ground into a common denominator.

11. To better the relationship between students and teachers, between parents and the schools, and among students.

12. To allow for the "late bloomer" (the student who, maturing late, is suddenly inspired to learn).

13. To reduce to the minimum classroom disciplinary problems.

14. To provide records of student work that actually mean something.

15. To prevent limiting a student's progress to one level during a school year.

16. To establish a realistic guidance program.

17. To reduce educational frustration and boredom for student and teacher alike.

18. To make administration of these goals easily possible in any school.

Chapter II
A Child in a Maze Called Education

Case studies of problems in individualizing education • Weaknesses of various methods designed for individualizing: heterogeneous grouping, homogeneous grouping, programmed study, open classroom concept, accountability, performance contracting, voucher system, track system, government programs

Albert's father is transferred by his company to another state in the middle of the school year. Such a move is often upsetting to a child. He leaves familiar surroundings and must make new friends and adjust. Albert, an intelligent student, is in his senior year of studies. He takes his high school transcript to the guidance counselor in his new school and asks to be scheduled into the same courses. The English classes are separated by ability on the basis of a child's past performance. In order to assign Albert to a physics class, the counselor, because of scheduling difficulties, has to place him in an English class for poor students. His parents appeal to the administrator for help, but there is no solution. In order to be scheduled into an English class at his proper level, he will have to drop physics. The school is not large enough to offer all levels of courses for every class period of the school day.

Academically Joan is not a good student. She realizes that college will be too difficult for her, but she wants to finish school and find a job working with small children in a recreational program or as an aid in a kindergarten or a day care center. Her problem is that she must fulfill the course requirements to receive a diploma. Those include a course in U.S. history and four units in English. In order to get these units she registers for a course that is defined as a pictorial review of the history of the United States. Students will view slides and movies and take field trips. Her English course is another "crip" called "The Unknown"—a pseudonymous title that signals to students (who quickly dub it "Boo! Lit") that here is another assured credit to hasten them through high school. Joan is miserable; none of her friends are in these classes. Discipline is poor when there is a congregation of students who have little direction or purpose. The teacher spends most of his time keeping order and trying to give some justification for the course's existence.

Chipper is an average student who becomes a victim of one of the largest upheavals the public schools have had. Organizing classrooms by ability is out; emphasis must be on social adjustment and "relativism," whatever that means. Teachers have to change their style of teaching, study new materials, and attend workshops to learn how to work with students under this new concept. They find that it is necessary to teach to one level while ignoring the others. The level taught will depend upon the teacher. In most classes slow students receive attention, leaving the rest to plod on their own. This is called independent study. "Contracting" becomes popular at this time. A student "contracting" for an "A" will have to complete a certain number of assignments and an additional project. To earn a "B," one must complete a fewer number of assignments and no project, and so on down the grade scale, the requirements decreasing in number. Chipper "contracts" for a "C" because it does not demand passing an exam. There is no range of grades within the contract levels. Chipper hands in the required *quantity* of assignments and gets by.

These pitiable yet archetypical cases—every teacher who reads this book could cite a dozen similar ones—could not occur under the Ramseur System.

From the beginning of our careers as teachers, we, too, felt that reaching the individual child was a primary goal. In order to develop a plan that would mean something to student and teacher alike, that would be acceptable to parents and administratively feasible, we first analyzed what we felt were the weaknesses in many of the existing educational policies.

How does one handle hordes of young people from every walk of life, cultural background, and academic capacity? The two stratagems most commonly resorted to are "homogeneous" or "heterogeneous" classrooms. Organizing children heterogeneously is to assign them to classes without regard to ability. This is glowingly described as "melting pot" education, but it is in our opinion a major factor in education going to pot. Proponents contend that heterogeneous classrooms accustom students to the differences in one another, whether social or racial, protect them from academic discrimination, and permit them to work with and learn from each other. All this may be so, but congregating children who are diverse in achievement, skills, rates of learning, cognitive styles, attitudes, and values can open up a can of worms. The instructor teaches the "average" and deprives both the bright and slow students of the special attention they need. Grading is emptied of meaning. The intellectually superior child will usually receive the highest marks without effort while the slow student will continue to fail or be given a low grade because he is competing against the mean of the whole class instead of against students of similar ability.

Some educators advocate seating the brighter students in heterogeneous classes together, in a bunch, or in other ways separating the quick from the less so, working with each category in shifts. This may be convenient, but the children are aware of the intellectual attribution made to them and their fellows regardless of such guises as designating the different classifications with names of flowers, birds, letters, numbers, etc. As a result, some students feel that the attribution itself defines them either as failures or successes, and they tend to accommodate themselves to the image. This may have a happy effect for the able student but not so happy for the slow one.

Homogeneous grouping is the assigning of students to different classes according to their intellectual capacity as determined by past performance and standardized test scores. Once popular, it has now been prohibited by the Supreme Court as discriminatory. Yet of the two methods, heterogeneous and homogeneous, the latter would seem to be the more felicitous in preparing the student for college or a vocation. Students are placed in a class of high, average, or low achievers by standardized achievement test scores, I.Q., grades, and teacher recommendations. Ideally, each child is taught at the level suited to him and is not forced to compete with students of greater or lesser ability; however, scheduling and inadequate data for classification sometimes pose insurmountable obstacles that result in the misplacement of children. The majority of the schools of this nation, because of a lack of funds (the flow of government money has not trickled far enough *down* to provide for more teachers and, thereby, smaller classes), must assign from twenty-five to thirty students to a class, but bright kids and slow kids do not come in administratively desirable lots of just so many this and just so many that. And another grave disadvantage is that one child may progress in his education at an accelerated rate during a certain period and then level off, while another student may advance slowly in the earlier years of schooling and then, for a variety of reasons, even within a single semester, suddenly spurt. Homogeneous grouping does not accommodate itself to such oscillations. Also, teachers may accept students as they are represented by cumulative folder materials. If a child is classified as a high or low achiever based upon past records and does not perform in the same manner at the next level or in a different subject, the teacher may adjust his opinion to that indicated by the child's most recent record. Either way, the child is subject to erroneous and prejudicial evaluation. He may have been an eager beaver in the eighth grade, perhaps raising expectations for him too highly; he may slump in the ninth grade, with the effect of dropping those expectations too radically. No real pulse of his abilities is being taken, and changes of temperature, perhaps temporary, are either ignored or taken too seriously. The Ramseur System, as we will show, avoids these pitfalls.

The preferred method today is some variation of homogeneous grouping that delicately evades thunder from the Supreme Court. "Programmed study," "open classrooms," "accountability," "performance contracting," "voucher system," the "track system," and others, have all been tried to locate the student in the educational maze and teach him, the "whole child" (every bit of him), what he needs at the time of discovery.

What are these strategies, how do they differ from each other, and where do they fail? Programmed study, advocated by B. F. Skinner, provides "immediate reinforcement." This means you get an M & M or you do not. If a student answers a question correctly, he is rewarded (reinforced) with candy or a smile from the instructor and given another question. Some programmed studies are in workbook form; others require mechanical aids, such as television monitors and recorders that ask questions for the student to answer on tape. There is also the talking typewriter (student pecks out an answer; if correct, the typewriter taps out another question, etc.) and many more. Each student moves through the programmed material at his own rate. The idea of teaching and learning through "immediate reinforcement" has even been extended to attendance. A school in Florida (as reported on a recent newscast) rewarded truant students with T-shirts or frisbees, whichever they preferred, if they would come to school. The goal of some educators seems to be how many students can be "schooled" rather than how many can be educated.

Of all the different strategies for personalizing education, programmed study probably comes closest because its approach is on a one-to-one basis—student-to-instructor or student-to-machine. But it is more effective in some subjects than it is in others, and in our opinion should be considered as an optional method available within a system—not as a system in itself. Some proponents of "programmed study" insist that materials can be designed to train the student in all subjects. However, we have observed that the materials for this method are not designed to allow the teaching of language, which is so badly needed. Moreover, they do not take into consideration the different styles in which students learn. Another drawback is the cost of the teaching machines and other paraphernalia, which is such that the average school likely hasn't the funds either to purchase or maintain the amount of equipment for all those children who could benefit. Nor is the average school likely to boast an adequate faculty, because one teacher cannot effectively supervise several children working at the same time on different machines with different materials. Some students, we might add, seem to view any sort of machine as an object to be dismantled, and not only are their teachers untrained in how to use machines to best effect, but few, besides, are convinced of the value of the approach itself. Perhaps their major objection—and ours—is the student-to-machine rather than the student-to-student relationship. Visualizing a future of children isolated in booths punching buttons, sensitive voices warn that the concept is too impersonal. Like so much to the taste of B. F. Skinner, it is Orwellian.

The open classroom is a relatively new concept of getting through to the individual child. It has not had a great following. The open classroom is, in fact, OPEN—no walls—where students are supposed to be part of the whole. The cliché: from the "whole child" to the "whole school." We suppose the planned confusion of this football stadium approach is intended to create a sense of "togetherness" and "belonging" among students. In theory—and some educators profess, in reality—the student in a history class that is held where other classes are also being conducted will not be distracted. Although pursuing their special interests together, students are treated as individuals and not as members of the total group. The teacher becomes a partner and a guide in the business of learning; he is the director or reinforcer of educational achievement.[1] A materials center has to be provided; a staff or aides must be employed to help the teacher tend to each child's needs; and an "open space" is, of course, essential. So, tear down the walls; if the school happens not to be constructed in a way that allows for easy flattening of partitions, build a new building; and if the open-space concept for some inexplicable reason fails to accomplish its purposes, build new walls.

We tried, once, to keep an open mind to this approach, but in keeping an open mind, as the adage goes, you have to take care that your brains don't fall out; with the open classroom concept your care is that your students don't fall out. Children who are easily distracted by noise and much moving around (and who isn't?) find "open space" education very disconcerting. Their teachers are not less disconcerted, as anyone will understand who has tried to explain Pythagoras' theorem to one crowd of distrustful students while another crowd to the left sings "Frère Jacques" and a third crowd to the right is chanting "Jeremiah was a Bullfrog." We have, moreover, a fundamental objection to this strategy for individualizing education. Though the teacher conceived as a partner may be sentimentally appealing to the general public, many students as well as professionals question the wisdom of this

posture for the instructor. John Holt asks, "Is it possible that our modern way of teaching, all gentleness,
persuasiveness, and human contact, tends to make
children get themselves and their work all mixed up?"[2]
We think so.

Accountability, a third strategy for individualizing
education, is vague and hard to define. It has a
threatening sound—if the schools' products (no specific numbers given) are inferior (no explanation or
guidelines for quality), someone is in trouble (also not
described, but the teacher can guess who). This
method is obsessed with behavioral objectives that the
teacher is directed to prepare for every student:
Johnny will learn to spell three words in one day
(objective); Johnny spells three words in one day (behavior). Teacher taught—student learned—everyone
is happy—except the teacher, who must write up all
the objectives for a hundred or more students each day.
Furthermore, the simpler the tasks she asks her students to perform, the better they will score, pleasing
her superiors. The children may learn nothing, but the
teacher has done what he was told to do!

A fourth strategy, performance contracting, brings
Chipper back into our story. The student "contracts"
for a grade and the grade tends to reflect quantity of
work rather than quality. This method is more commonly practiced in colleges, but it has been percolating
down into the secondary schools, another means of
hastening the student from grade to grade and thence
out into the cold, hard world, where others can assume
the responsibility for his future whether or not he has
actually learned anything that might help him earn a
living. Performance contracting is a cheat and a delusion. It is shameful.

The voucher system hasn't really gotten off the ground. This idea places much of the responsibility for a child's education on the parents. Parents are presented with a voucher (based on the amount of money that the local and state governments allocate for the education of each school age child) that serves as payment for the child's education in the school the parents choose. It sounds good, but such free choice can invite a host of problems for the public school system. Who, for example, will provide financial support for schools that draw few students? Are they to close? What will happen to those schools that offer a strong academic program and draw a plethora of students, but of widely varying abilities? How will they be handled? What about the child who cannot meet stringent academic standards but whose abilities are higher than the level taught in academically inferior schools? Where is that child to go? And, finally, what would the government do if, as a consequence of free choice, schools become once again *de facto* segregated? It's a long way from Boston to Montgomery, Alabama, for Judge Garrity to order out the buses. The voucher system, appealing as it may be, won't work.

The track system was abolished in Washington, D.C. by the decision of U.S. Circuit Court of Appeals Justice James S. Kelly Wright in 1968.[3] If, then, "tracking" is out, why bother mentioning it? Because, though tracking is technically outlawed, pressure to "detrack" the curriculum has not been applied equally to all schools, and many continue operating some form of the system. (The strategies we have discussed above are attempts to track within the law.) Under this plan, which is the simplest and most conventional method of guiding children through their education, a student chooses a field of study and a level within that field. This is his "track." If, based upon prior school performance and standardized test scores, he qualifies for his chosen track, he will spend the next four years in it—unless he switches or fails to make the grades. He may not remain in some of the subjects of one track and take subjects in another track. The track for college-bound students offers units in foreign languages, advanced sciences, etc.; the vocational track emphasizes job training; and there is a track for students with learning difficulties. An experience in human tolerance and compassion is lost when these children are separated into sheep and goats, and those branded as goats never get the chance to benefit from interaction with the sheep.

Tracking inevitably results in segregation. Black students make up the largest percentage of those in the lower track, and *de facto* segregation once again takes place within the integrated schools if homogeneous grouping is practiced. Problems rising out of such organization of classes have erupted into violence in many public schools. Although outlawed, "tracking" continues in one form or another and is covered by a variety of euphemisms, and the quandary of how to educate a disparate student body persists.

None of these strategies has proved satisfactory. Educators continue to search for a technique that will teach the individual yet not separate him from other students; one that will expose him to different social, racial, religious, and economic backgrounds without compromising the quality of the education that he receives. The dilemma has become a windfall for bureaucrats, whose solutions well-nigh paralyze the schools. In fact, so much public attention has been focused in the last decade on finding a workable method of teaching to the individual child, and so much tax money has been poured into it, it's no wonder that education has become a profitable field for the ambitious person seeking fame, money, or a way out of the classroom to an office with an impressive title. From these medicine men more snake oil has been bought as a tonic for this or that malady of the public schools than the average parent would believe. Any classroom teacher, however, will recognize the scenario related here.

It is announced that a new program with full funding from the federal government will become a part of the school curriculum next year. Teachers are to report to their school, or some central point, two weeks before the fall semester starts to be trained to carry it out. If they are lucky, they may receive a stipend of fifteen dollars a day, which might defray the baby-sitting costs. They will be trained by someone with a fancy professional soubriquet but with little, if any, recent classroom experience; this expert, nevertheless, will be well versed in the latest educational jargon (not ordinarily used by classroom teachers, who do not have time to learn it and who would have few places to use it if they did). The program this expert expounds is going to accomplish all the miracles that all the others failed to. He is paid generously to prove this to the teachers, who sit in obliged attention to the workshop while wishing they were free for the rest of that unpaid vacation in order to gear themselves for the task of the coming year. They will do as they are told, and they will not assert their opinions nor question the wisdom of the method nor refuse to be a part of it. They are not there to be consulted, goodness no! They have been

summoned to receive wisdom from on high. If, however, some intrepid teacher is foolhardy enough, he
may raise an objection . . . only to be told that there is a
long waiting list for vacancies in the school, or that he
can be transferred somewhere else. Not many teachers
are financially independent. Few of us are made of the
stuff of heroes. The bold dissenter submits and dreams
of being again a student, when he was treated with
more tender respect for his sensibilities.

We begin the school year. A month after school starts
the director finally gets around to pretesting students
assigned to the latest wonder method. Several months
after that an investigator from the federal government
decides that the color scheme in the classrooms needs
improving, and children are shuffled to satisfy a racial
quota. Half the year is over, and we are still trying to
get the program started. So much time is consumed in
testing children and filling out questionnaires that
little is left for teaching and learning. Students rebel.
They refuse to be tested. And, teachers, who are by
now themselves bordering on mutiny, are hanged if
they will fill out forms whose questions are personal to
the point of downright invasion of their privacy and
that of their charges.

Whenever we feel inclined to indulge in righteous
indignation, there's one federally-funded brainstorm
that we recall with special affection. It was supposed to
improve reading. Without going into detail, what it did
better was to cure students and their teachers of in-
somnia. Nell, a tenth grader, is assigned to one of the
special classes. She immediately realizes that she is
being pointed out as a slow student, and she resents
the stigma. She and her parents request that she be
transferred to another class. This, they are informed,
cannot be done. Nell knows that she must study hard

to learn her subjects, but she is conscientious about her work. Her grades in science begin to fall because she has had to miss classes on several occasions to be tested for the reading program. When she refuses to be tested any more and asks that she be allowed to return to her science class, she is told that she will not be forced to take the test but that if she won't, no science either. She must spend the period in the office. Teachers, students, and many of the parents complained, to no avail. Down our throats was this seizure of bureaucratic officiousness stuffed. Some students preferred being punished for cutting the classes to attending them, because the waste of time was transparent to everyone. Students were obliged to fill out a report each week on what they had received in the way of exercises for that period. This was just one of many tedious requirements, but, remember, these students had been singled out for the course because they were poor readers. And what questions did they—who could scarcely puzzle out "See Jane jump"—get to struggle with? *How many hours [have you had] of multi-media teaching? How many hours of tutorial help?* The children understood nothing.

We teachers who had been dragooned into the program were plagued with questionnaires also. One set of them really stuck in our craw. We were required to complete a self-evaluation and an evaluation of our students. When the questions weren't asinine, they were prurient and meretricious. We were asked, if white, did we like blacks, and, if black, did we care for whites. We were asked whether we were happier teaching before or after integration. Then we were asked to judge our students' feelings about race, and whether these feelings were positive or negative, and so forth. Black or white, many of us balked indignantly. This was an arrant invasion of privacy, and it was indefensible that we, teachers, were being required to cast a value judgment on the attitudes of our students. We said we would not answer those particular questions and would not sign our names to the forms. We were told that would be all right; but a few days later, the authorities brought the evaluation sheets back to those of us who had refused to complete them, demanding that we do so. We were stunned. Our names, remember, had been removed. How was it known which sheet belonged to which teacher?

To us, the experience was terrifying. Had the government established a net of informers feeding private information about us to our superiors?

If you are wondering what all this probing had to do with reading—so wondered we! But with our rebellion over the evaluation forms, students and teachers thought it would all come to an end. The program was a monstrous flop. But we were in due course informed via the news media that the program had been a roaring success, with "significant" figures (?!) to prove it, and that it was being refunded by the federal government for the coming school year. Furthermore, everybody was so pleased with this trial project that the program was scheduled for expansion to those unfortunate schools in the area that had been deprived from partaking of the miracle.

The realities don't matter. Get ready for more workshops!

Footnotes, Chapter II

[1]Joseph W. Davis, "The Open Classroom: A Challenging Concept," *South Carolina Education Journal,* (Fall, 1970), p. 14.

[2]John Holt, *How Children Fail* (New York: Pittman Publishing Corporation, 1964), p. 43. Holt questions, "is it not possible that the old fashioned way had merit . . . did not know whether teachers like me or not . . . work was what concerned teachers . . . if good (work) commended and if bad it was criticized. Maybe it was easier for children to grow up in a world in which, when they impinged on the world of adults, they were treated firmly, impersonally, and ceremoniously, but were otherwise left alone." p. 43.

[3] Hobson vs. Hinson #269 F. Supp. 401 (D.D.C. 1967) off'd sub nom Smuck vs. Hobson, 408 F. 2 d 175 (D.C.C. 1969).

Chapter III
A Guide to the Maze

Design of RPL • Random assignment of students to a class • Involvement of teacher, parent and child • Respect for privacy of child (no study of previous records) • Method of individualizing in RPL classes • Involvement of all children of all levels in classwork • Movement from one group to another • Preparation for child's first choice • Restrictions on changes from group to group • Student-teacher conferences • Provisions for the handicapped • Adaptability of RPL (ease of implementation)

In designing our technique, we considered two criteria as most important: first, it must be easy to implement; and second, it must be inexpensive. The Ramseur System poses no scheduling difficulties and requires no additional personnel or special materials.

The students in the Ramseur program are randomly assigned to a class. In other words, a child registers for a course and is assigned to a given class of that course by computer or by a counselor—he is not placed according to his prior performance. Each class, therefore, contains a wide range of intellectual abilities, socioeconomic backgrounds, and other differences.

Parents receive a letter explaining RPL, notifying them that their child is in the system, and requesting their interest and cooperation; and they are asked to sign and return it. The letter serves as a protection for the teacher as well as for the student. A father whose son was in an RPL English class irately asked the teacher why his boy's poor performance in that subject had not been reported until late in the semester. The teacher reminded him that the letter he had received informed parents that all work was in the student's subject file, and that the file could be used not only by the student for study but also by his parents for a continuous review of their child's progress. The father, as so often happens, had no memory of the letter, which he had signed without reading.

In addition to the letter informing parents of what their children will be doing, the whole RPL system, including the within-class method of grouping, type of assignments, and grading of work, is explained to the class. Everybody—teacher, parent, and child—knows what he is getting into.

RPL teachers, contrary to the practice of most educators, do not review the cumulative folder of a student's past record at the beginning of their association with him unless they need information about some physical or emotional handicap that would seriously affect his learning or that of the others in the class. Teachers, being human, may be influenced by records that purport to show what the child is capable or incapable of doing. Since RPL teachers consult the academic and disciplinary records only when the student continues to do poorly in a particular class,[1] no student needs to feel pretagged in any RPL course.

We, along with many other teachers, believe that the child should feel free to establish a new record for himself in each class and that he has a right to decide what he wants to reveal about himself. The RPL teacher resists the American lust for probing into everything about a person in order to psychoanalyze

him with the hope of curing him, laying him bare
and defenseless before society for reasons of idle and
salacious curiosity. At an RPL school, the student may
be secure in the knowledge that no one knows anything about him except what he wishes to be known.
The student, not the teacher, draws his own picture.

Three levels of learning are offered in the academic
and vocational disciplines. We designate these levels
as *groups.* The primary level, Group 3, requires the
student to exercise cognition and leads the student to
divergent and convergent thinking and to simple
evaluation of information gained through study, classroom lecture, and discussion. *Cognition* is the act of
knowing; a child's cognitive abilities at one age become part of later cognitive abilities. He knows
round, a ball is round, it rolls, a wheel is also round
and it rolls—things that are round roll. A fact in history, English, math, etc. is learned, and then it is
expanded—a fact leads to another fact or to similar
facts. To *diverge,* one goes from a common point, i.e.,
fact to generalities or different opinion of that fact. To
converge, the student is led from generalities to
specifics, i.e., a common point—the reverse of diverg-
ing. This leads to evaluation of knowledge. Learning
facts, incorporating them into a body of knowledge,
and having that information further explained and
expanded by lectures from the teacher will aid students in all groups to understand subject content.
Group 3 students in all classes except English are not
graded on their ability to write, but they are encouraged to learn as much about composition as they are
able through classroom participation in all assignments and especially through classroom and group
discussion. All tests for this group are objective. The

questions and statements are expressed with the simplest vocabulary in order to reach the lowest level. If a student has a serious reading problem, he will take the Group 3 test in class with the other students and later, in private, a similar one orally. Achievement at Group 3 level means minimum competency.[2] (Discussed in more detail under evaluation).

Group 2 students, taking the same class with Group 3, are required to practice writing. Questions on their tests demand answers in essay form, and composition as well as knowledge of subject matter are the basis for grading. Single words, phrases, and incomplete sentences are not acceptable. The student must learn to answer a question so that the question is understood in the introduction of the answer. Example: What claim did Harold Hardrada, King of Norway, have to Edward the Confessor's throne? Answer: Harold Hardrada, King of Norway, made claim to Edward the Confessor's throne on the grounds of . . . etc.[3] Students in this group will learn to be brief and clear in their written work. Various fields of learning use a different vocabulary and style of writing. Research, problem-solving, relationships, inference, and the need for recall are significant in Group 2 study.

Group I students, on the other hand, are given more intensive and extensive assignments to be done outside class, and tests for these students require broader knowledge and independent analysis. All three groups are offered some independent study. One of the important features of RPL is that the schedule of assignments has been arranged so that the students are together more often than they are apart. The only time that students may not be working together is during independent study periods and periods for review of a

unit of study before a test. Independent study should
serve a specific purpose, should be planned with the
librarian, and should not be used as a means of dumping students on her while the teacher works with
others, or just "goofs off," tempting though the prospect may be. During independent study periods, some
students may remain in the classroom for special
tutoring while others work under the librarian's eye.

When material is to be reviewed, the teacher, with
permission from the librarian, may say to his class, "If
any of you can use this time for something more beneficial, you may go to the library or stay here and
tackle something else." No group is held for a
review—the individual decides what he needs.

Assignments, reading, writing, or a test, are given
for all the class in a general announcement. No project,
seating arrangement, or instruction excludes or points
out a given group. All classroom work includes all
three groups, and at no time is a child identified before
his classmates as belonging to one or another. Certain
subjects do not lend themselves to Group 3 level. For
example, advanced courses in math and science, third
and fourth year foreign language classes, and English
composition are designed for those who have already
acquired the basic skills; teachers, however, have
found that Group 2 as well as Group I can benefit from
these advanced courses.

The student chooses the group in which he wishes to
work. He may move from level to level as his needs and
desires dictate. In order to aid a youngster when he is
ill or when he participates in a school function that
would place an extraordinary burden on him, RPL
permits dropping to a lower group for the time being.
RPL teachers establish course requirements for each

group. For instance, the student who moved to a lower level because of illness must, if he returns to the higher level, fulfill some requirement at that level for the course. It is true that catching-up won't be easy, but if he has the ability and determination, he will be able to complete the requirements. These standards, however, should be designed to promote continuous progress and not discourage late entrance into a higher group. Such flexibility prepares the child to make hard decisions; he knows that when he wants to and feels he's ready, he can go for broke. He knows that trying for a higher level of education will cost him in time and effort, and that he may not make it. There's no shame or penalty attached to failure; no one but he, his parents, and the teacher knows of his valiant attempt; but there it is, he may work like a dog and still not make it. And this is the way is should be: nothing to put an artificial lid on ambition, but the risk of defeat ever-present no matter how hard he may try. Educators have too often designed curriculums that allow every child every advantage without corresponding sacrifice, a condition contrary to reality and basic common sense. In the RPL system the student's responsible freedom provides him with the opportunity of earning his way. It permits him to develop at his own rate and come realistically to terms with what he can and cannot accomplish.

Although an explanation of any system is necessary for students to comprehend what will be happening to them, few will take the account seriously or fully understand it until they are actually engaged in the program. RPL teachers present the first unit of a course as a model of what is to come—demonstrating what will be learned in the unit of work (say, a chapter in a textbook or a period of history), explaining the basic materials (dates, terms, the plot of a story and what fiction is), and guiding class discussion. At the end of this unit, all students take tests on all three levels, Groups 1, 2, and 3. The teacher grades these, returns them to the students, and explains the questions and their grading. In this way, every student has information on all three groups and, by experience, now knows what is expected and how his work will be judged.

All papers are annotated to explain the mistakes and suggest other or better ways of presenting material. Points taken off are defined. Example: If there is a -8 in the margin and three of those points were lost in errors of composition, this loss will be defined with the symbol -3c placed above the -8 to show exactly the value of each point in the answer. This may seem complicated, but it is not in practice, and it can be most helpful.

A boy named Joby failed to pass history at Group 2 level. His mother, Mrs. Hill, ambitious for him, was convinced the system or the teacher were at fault, not Joby. The notation of errors on his papers indicated that few points had been lost because of mistakes in composition; Joby had failed because he did not know his history. To verify this conclusion, the teacher asked Joby to take his tests in Groups 2 and 3 for one reporting period. (Group 3 requires no writing skills.) He failed in both. The teacher asked for a conference with the mother, who came, daggers drawn, to defend her child. But after reviewing his work, Mrs. Hill admitted that it was obvious that Joby was not studying and, therefore, could not pass in any group. True, he possessed a skill that many students find difficult to acquire, but one that he used to express nothing. Joby finished the course with a B^2. No doubt his mother decided he would by golly hit the books, and he obliged. He had no excuses, which his file proved. We feel that any form of test should be an additional educational tool and not just a means of arriving at a grade.

After presentation of the first unit of material, testing, and evaluation, the student will use this information to make his first choice of group. Discussion and review of all levels of work with the entire class continue throughout the course so that a student considering a move from one to another has a clear picture upon which to base his decision. His moves need follow no particular pattern. He may change after each reporting period if he wishes; he may bypass a group in either direction; or he may remain in one group for the duration of the course. This freedom allows him to learn at a pace he can control.

Certain restrictions have been placed on changes from group to group in order to prevent students from manipulating the system in order to "coast" for a pleasant while (using the system to negate the purpose of the system). Though the liberty RPL students enjoy to elect their preferred level is granted so that they may learn to assume responsibility without suffering academic penalties for their honest mistakes in judgment, RPL also teaches students that they must make decisions thay they believe in and sincerely hope to be permanent—a training that will be vital to them as adults. To accomplish this—to protect the student from misusing his freedom—we established the following conditions:

1. He must remain in a given group for at least two reporting periods and take the final exam in it before he can qualify for a yearly or final grade in that group.

2. He must spend the last reporting period in the

group in which he expects to earn his final grade. This requirement is to prevent him from moving down in order to preserve a grade and "goof-off" the last period.

3. In addition to the requirement of the two or more reporting periods in a group, the student must fulfill any course assignments of a particular level. RPL teachers assign course projects *at the beginning of the school year.* (We'll explain in Chapter VII why this is important.) In order to assure a student that he will not be handicapped in moving from one group to another, the projects assigned to a lower group form part of the project required in a higher group. A project for Group 3 is the first step in completing a project for Group 2, and the two projects are included in the requirement for Group I.

At the end of every reporting period, RPL teachers confer with each student. The graded work, which is kept in the student's file, serves as an important basis for counseling during these conferences. This is the course file where all papers, annotated and graded, are kept along with the introductory letter that parents have signed and presumably read also. A review of this file is of immeasurable help in advising the student and aiding him in planning for the next reporting period. *Regardless of the advice given by the teacher,* however—and this we want to emphasize again and again—*the actual choice of work level must be the student's and parents'.* If he wishes to advance into a group that the teacher feels is too difficult for him, he may be counseled against the change; but the final decision is made by him and can be changed only upon the insistence of a parent.[4]

RPL teachers have cautioned against advancing to a higher level many times only to be proved wrong in their analysis of the student's ability. This happens because the RPL student is working with others of similar ability as well as different capacities and is therefore strongly motivated to try for a new and higher goal. If his reach exceeds his grasp, *there is no academic penalty inflicted upon him;* he can take pride in his willingness to take on a challenge, even though ultimately it bests him. We can't all high jump 7'9", but it's better and more fun to try than not. And one bad jump isn't the end of everything in the Ramseur System. A child can at any time he wishes try again, and this new effort may be successful. No one has in the meantime misplaced him; no one has labeled him or directed pejorative attention to his weaknesses. Under RPL, the student *paints his own image* and *designs his own future.* He must, of course, assume the responsibility for that image.

It is a deplorable fact, and no longer a secret, that many students in secondary schools today can neither read nor write. It is also true that many physically, mentally, and emotionally handicapped children are being treated within the public schools without the aid of specialists or special materials. When help is provided for handicapped students, it is in many cases limited because the funds aren't there. Some educators and parents strongly protest the mixing of handicapped students with "normal" children. Serious problems can arise from such blending. The handicapped child may be ridiculed, embarrassed, even physically hurt; or conversely, he may be a problem himself if, unable to control his emotions, he reacts to some situations violently. Baiting of the handicapped or disturbances that they are solely responsible for take place not so much in the classroom as in the halls, on the grounds, in school buses, and during extra-curricular activities, especially at secondary level. To excuse the mentally or emotionally troubled for their transgressions is bad policy: if the rest of the school population does not understand that these students have special problems, they naturally assume that they are receiving preferential treatment; but to explain is to point the handicapped out as "different." The dilemma can be anguishing. If the school is large, the faculty cannot personally know all the children and cannot afford to treat them differently in disciplinary matters. Furthermore, handicapped as they may be emotionally or mentally, at this secondary school age they are fast becoming young adults; and their physical strength, coupled with their instability, can combine for a disruptive, even dangerous, situation. RPL does not eradicate the problem of these children outside the classroom. However, as you will see, RPL grouping helps alleviate it.

Group 4 was added to our technique in the school year of 1970-71. A Group 4 student is one who has failed to keep up at Group 3 level. He may be clinically handicapped or he may be so far behind in basic learning skills—the jargon is sometimes hard to avoid— that he cannot pass at competency level—we failed again! Under RPL, however, such a child can remain in a regular class and enjoy the companionship and stimulus of his coevals. The hope is that he will be able to receive special help outside the classroom so that, if possible, he is able to regain some of his "lost" education. The records of all students who have failed to show progress at the end of the first semester (in yearly courses) or at the end of a nine-weeks' period (for

semester courses) are reviewed by a guidance counselor, whose duty it is to be familiar with the cumulative folder containing a student's records, in order to
guide children into the right subjects and help them
obtain information about colleges and available jobs.
If the folder indicates that inherent inability to learn,
emotional instability, or some physical handicap have
impeded progress and will probably prevent the child
from getting along in Group 3, he may be offered work
in Group 4.[5]

This level is never discussed before a class: only a
Group 4 student is aware that it exists. Before placement, the teacher requests a conference with the student's parents to explain their child's problem and the
purpose of Group 4. With the agreement of the parent,
the student is then offered the option. The manner in
which the teacher discusses the purposes and benefits
of this level is vital to the child's acceptance of the
program and of himself as a participant. A Group 4
student continues to take Group 3 tests. During independent study, he works on projects designed especially for him by his teacher. A few Group 4 students
have, in the past, begun to perform in the Group 3
work they continued to do in class and have finished
the term with credit at that level. We can only specu-
late on the reason for this improvement, but it is possible that relief from both work pressure and the fear
of never-ending failure liberates the child's mental
faculties.

Important features of Group 4 are the following:

1. *A student cannot himself select Group 4.* The decision is first the teacher's.

2. *Parents must be consulted:* they must approve.

3. *Academic failure alone may not determine the decision.* The underlying cause of the student's troubles is the criterion.

4. *The student* receives all available help for his special problems; but he *continues attending his regularly assigned classes.* Further attention to him can be given during independent study periods.

Richard E. Gross observed, "We have long known that the students in any class have more differences than likenesses;"[6] it is therefore imperative that any educational technique allow for those differences. Under RPL, failure is no longer frightening because it can be avoided or overcome, or, importantly, accepted as a sign post to another, more rewarding direction. The administrators of the Camden school, at the time when RPL was first instituted, had reservations about giving students such freedom, fearing that they might opt for the routes of least resistance. Contrary to this apprehension, a majority of students choose the more difficult work. Students have their own goals in life and are inclined to reject being programmed by adults. Given the choice, they will, in most cases, challenge themselves.

This system does not need directors, co-directors, offices, special equipment, or staffs. It requires a filing cabinet, special grade sheets (which can be printed in the school), and a teacher who knows his subject, who is willing to contribute extra but rewarding hours, and who does not mind risking his reputation by making his work available to those who are authorized to study his teaching and evaluation of students. RPL can work with and alongside any established educational program. An ideal school, however, would be one in which the whole faculty is trained in the Ramseur

System, but RPL teachers have to be those who choose of their own free will to accept the exacting standards. Not every teacher will. It's a matter of dedication.

Footnotes, Chapter III

[1] This method of aiding the student is explained under guidance and not explained in detail here to avoid unnecessary repetition. The steps are, however, explained to the student in the introduction.

[2] The most recent concern is the revelation that many students throughout the nation are graduating from schools without having acquired the basic skills. Acting on this discovery, states are designing competency tests to administer to all students before they may receive a diploma. Offered here is the solution in Group 3 standards.

[3] King Harold Hardrada of Norway made claim to Edward the Confessor's throne on the grounds that he was a direct descendant of Canute, King of England.

[4] This will continue to hold true until the U.S. Supreme Court rules that parents have no right to be guardians of their children's education as they now cannot guard the morals of their children.

[5] Failures because of lack of productivity or absenteeism are not considered.

[6] Richard E. Gross, "Individualizing Instruction for Students of Different Abilities," *Teaching the Social Studies What, Why and How,* (Scranton, Pennsylvania: International Textbook Company, 1969), p. 423.

Chapter **IV**
Finding the Individual in the Maze

*Reaching the child in a heterogeneous group
• Segregating without discriminating • Making the
differences in children a stimulus to learning
• General pattern of classroom instruction: introduction of unit of study, presentation of elementary
material, the lecture, discussion, review and lead-in
to new unit*

Reaching each individual child and preparing him for
what is styled a "healthy life adjustment" by having
him work alongside (and learn from) many other children of every imaginable background is at best a
difficult goal, confronting public schools with major
obstacles. The conventional or experimental existing
systems (voucher, track, programmed study, etc.), as
we have seen, are flawed. They tend, besides, to contradict one another. Too often, any attempt to congre-
gate students heterogeneously results in a form of
mass production that stifles against getting the best
out of every boy or girl, no two of whom are alike.

We can put a million pieces of steel through identical
processes, and get a million identical finished products,
because every piece of steel we start with is identical. In
preparing the minds of children, however, we are working
with a million different pieces of raw material. Considering this fact, we do an amazingly good job of turning

out semi-standardized minds, which, unfortunately, is exactly the reverse of what we should be doing.[1]

On the other hand, individualizing education requires some form of segregation according to ability —and there we are again, discriminating academically, often socially, and economically (the cultural advantages of relative affluence), and to all appearances, until a large black or hispanic middle class grows, racially and ethnically. And there is no question that we do harm to a child's perception of himself.

In constructing the Ramseur method, we asked ourselves the following questions: How to do what we wanted to do in a heterogeneous group without making distinctions and, thus, categorizing students either as inferior or superior? How could all capacity levels be taught with or without special materials, teacher aides, and flexible scheduling? The most important question was: Was is possible, in a single class, to teach students of disparate interests, intellects, and backgrounds and *make these differences a stimulus* for learning from others rather than what they so often are today, a deterrent to individual educational growth? To come up with answers, we realized that it was necessary first to analyze what was significant about such a classroom. Our conclusions were as follows:

1. A student *needs the stimulus* of other students of varied backgrounds if he is to relate what he learns in the classroom to the world he knows and if he is to have opened to him a world he does not know.

2. *Any subject has basic material of value and interest to all students* regardless of their prior social and educational experiences. Basic content normally in-

cludes empirical matter acquainting the student with the foundations of the subject.

3. *A simple vocabulary* to define and explain content is always appropriate and will make the subject understandable to the slow student, yet will *not* lose the superior student. Children today have taken it upon themselves to simplify their language, and, in many cases, have given new meaning to old words and phrases.

4. *Repetition of facts,* which can be unnecessary for the average and superior student, *does not aid the slow student.* Instead, it bores him as much as it does the better student and tends to make him withdraw.

5. *If a student does not have to fear placement and labeling, he will relax* and fling himself into classroom discussions and projects. This "belonging" will encourage him to expand his knowledge so that he may broaden his participation.

6. A student will learn a subject because it satisfies some desire he has for the present or future, because he enjoys competing with his classmates, or because he needs to "belong." *Rarely will he study for parents or teachers.*

7. *The teacher is important,* however, *as a guide, organizer, and dispenser of educational content.* If the teacher is to do his job, he must be granted the same freedom to be himself that his students enjoy.

8. *The teacher* in the classroom must have a *comprehensive knowledge* of his subject.

9. In addition to the teacher's own specialty, *he should be able to speak and write clearly and correctly.*

10. The teacher must be able to *maintain discipline* in his class in a manner that encourages participation by all students while preventing an atmosphere of orderly freedom from fragmenting into chaos.

RPL teachers explain the hierarchy of intellectual skills, and then demonstrate by discussion and questions how students may move from one level to another. Inductive and deductive learning are demonstrated by the presentation of small units of material and by questions at different levels. Teachers follow a general pattern in classroom instruction. There are differences in presentation that are necessary because of the nature of the subject. In general, the pattern of classroom instruction proceeds in the following manner:

First, the instructor introduces *the unit.* Why the unit is important, how the knowledge to be gained from it can be beneficial to the students, and how and when the unit material can be used in everyday life, are all explained. Second, *elementary material,* such as specific events or the names of important individuals, is extracted from the body of work and presented to the students as a springboard for understanding the entire unit. Students will be given a brief definition or description of this material. The student's mastery of such limited information is tested. At this point, he should have a general overview. He should know the basic empirical constituents of the unit and should be prepared to begin placing those facts in an order from which the whole content transpires—like putting the pieces of a puzzle together to see the whole picture.

The third step is *the lecture.* This traditional tool of pedagogy has lost favor in our public schools, but RPL teachers have not thrown it out. The lecture is a way of bringing material together—facts that relate to other facts, interacting facts, cause and effect—and of suggesting possible interpretations. Through the lecture the instructor reveals to the student the different modes of resolving questions, the possibility of dif-

ferent resolutions (not in math!), relation, and inference. This is the time when a teacher can be most
dynamic in expounding his subject. This is also when
he may reveal his incompetence—which may explain
the lecture's waning popularity. In our experience,
students want formal lectures, and many feel that
teachers who avoid giving them have abdicated their
responsibility. A trend in recent years has been to
delegate to the student the traditional duty of the
instructor, which is to teach the material. This is supposed to put student and teacher on the same level—
all friendliness and togetherness. Anyone who has
sat through a student's disorganized mumblings and
fumblings for thirty minutes or so knows how awful
such a travesty of instruction is.[2] Also, one wonders
with the students whether the teacher knows his
oats.

The fourth step in classroom teaching is *discussion*
following the lecture. (In courses such as mathematics,
this may include group or individual problem-
solving.) RPL class discussions are conducted in a re-
laxed manner, with the teacher serving as a moderator
to prevent any individual from dominating and also to
steer students back on course when they wander off
the topic. Very few RPL students fail to participate
after the first few weeks. Once they make the initial
foray out of silence, their confidence grows. The instructor cautions against oversensitivity by pointing
out that everybody, teachers included, will at times
make statements or ask questions that are redundant
or foolish. Since classes tend to react to their teacher's
attitude, the fear of being ridiculed can be removed.
Besides, we've found that children are more resilient
than they are given credit for. They withdraw and

refuse to interact with the class not from criticism, but from *unjustified* criticism. The number of class periods devoted to discussion depends upon the teacher's judgment of how much interest the subject continues to spark and the relative value.

Instructors under the Ramseur system have found that discussions are more effective in heterogeneous classes of fair size. When a student contributes to discussions or projects, it is important that he participates because he wishes to, not because he is forced to, and that he speaks not as a member of Group 1, 2, or 3, but as a member of the class.

The fifth and final step in classroom teaching is the *review, and the lead-in* from the completed unit to a new one.

Over the years, we have asked RPL graduates for written critiques of the system. The majority have expressed a preference for RPL grouping, stating that they feel they have worked harder and learned more from the interchange of ideas with fellow students of diverse interests and experience. This favorable reaction, we believe, is attributable to self-grouping that allows children to progress on a level that they can handle but that as the same time lets them share in all class work, regardless of the group they belong to. The percussionist in a symphony orchestra who sits most of the evening beside his triangle or cymbals, waiting for that one moment in the third movement when the score calls for him, is rated—graded—by the conductor on how well he performs then, and on nothing else: but he is meanwhile an integral part of the orchestra, enjoying and contributing to the great music. The Ramseur System exacts from each according to his ability, but it gives to all regardless.

Footnotes, Chapter IV

[1] From *Magnificent Delusion* by Fred G. Clark. Copyright ©
1940, McGraw/Hill Book Company, Inc. Used with permission of
McGraw/Hill Book Company.

[2] Universities and colleges are more guilty of this than the
public schools; however, this method of "teaching" is steadily
creeping into the lower grades. Furthermore, why should one pay
for or choose a course to be taught by a fellow student who also
came to learn from a professional?

Chapter V
Evaluation: A,B,C and 1,2,3

*Cases of unfair evaluation of students' work • The
teacher as evaluator • The meaning of evaluation
• The weakness in some of the present criteria for
most grading systems • The Ramseur System of
grading • Illustrations from RPL files • Reflec-
tions of intangibles in a student's performance
• Evaluation as a vital component of the teaching
and learning process*

Sue and Gregg are in the same history class. Sue, who
is very bright, enjoys studying, whereas Gregg, a slow
learner, is often frustrated in his work. The class is
heterogeneous; therefore, Mr. Carter has the task of
teaching history to students who range in ability from
"A" to "Z."

Unilluminated by the revelations of the Ramseur
System, he, poor man, separates his charges based on
records of previous performance. He names the groups
1, 2, 3 or red, white, and blue—which hoodwinks no
one, because everyone is fully aware what the numbers or colors signify. (A young fellow recently com-
mented to his mother that a certain girl in his class
was a "dummy." When asked why he had made such a
statement, he said, "She is in the yellow bird group and
they are the 'dummies'.") Mr. Carter will help one
bunch while another bunch is given desk assignments
or sent to a learning center to perform some task, often
"busy work."

Sue—bright as a button—knows that she will be required to do more work than slower students. Not illogically, she expects a better grade. And that's how it works out. She gets her A or B while the average group is sentenced to C− or C+, and poor Gregg, who would rather be hunting arrowheads on the sandy banks of the Wateree River than studying history,will get what is left over along with the stigma of being a "dummy." He has no way of avoiding that stigma because he of the yellow birds must sit with the other finches of the same color and peck at the crumbs that are scattered before them. He will have no exposure to more stimulating work; and, if his records were misleading, neither he nor his teacher will ever know the injustice done to him. Meanwhile, do you imagine Sue is delighted with her high marks? Quite the contrary. She is fed up; she cannot receive the attention she needs to challenge her bright and curious mind because poor Mr. Carter—who at this point would rather be hunting arrowheads himself—must disperse his time among three groups and cannot possibly give each the attention that all should be receiving. This harassed situation, to the surprise of no one, foments disciplinary problems. Someone should have told Mr. Carter of the Ramseur method, which for years has been successfully dealing with his predicament by devoting more, not less, time to each level, neither slowing the Sues nor ignoring and embarrassing the Greggs.

A favorite true anecdote from the early days of RPL, when it was first being introduced in Camden with few believers in the system, concerns a boy in a fourth grade class for low achievers. In charge was Miss Becky Milling,[1] who did not believe all of her students were slow. Miss Milling is one of those rare, wonderful

people who absolutely refuses to give up on any child;
reminding our editor of his mother, whom he caught on
her knees praying for Stalin's soul on the afternoon of
the announcement of the tyrant's welcome demise.
"Maw, how could you!" She replied (defensively), "Well,
he just might have repented at the last moment."

Anyhow, Miss Milling asked permission to give RPL
a try. She explained to her children how the system
operates, telling them that it was possible to be in
Group 1 in one subject and maybe in a different group
in another subject, that the choice was theirs, and that
they had no need to fear making a bad choice because
they could shift from group to group at the end of every
reporting period. They kept asking her if they really
could choose, finding this restoration of their dignity
hard to believe. The little boy—Jimmy—had never
made more than a 30 on a spelling paper, but he
averred as how he wanted to try Group 2 in that subject. Miss Milling did not discourage him. On the very
next spelling test, this certified dumb-dumb made 100.
He was eager to move to Group 1. She suggested that
he might be wise to stay in Group 2 a little longer to be
sure he could maintain a high grade. He said, "But
Miss Milling, I can spell stethoscope. I really can. Let
me spell it." She answered, "All right, Jimmy, but first
let me get a dictionary because I am not at all sure that
I know how to spell it myself."

Would Jimmy have been a Gregg in Mr. Carter's
classroom? Only two of the 27 students in Miss Milling's class were incapable of achieving above Group 3
in any subject, but even these two could salvage their
self-esteem by being able to say that *they* had chosen
that level, they had not been relegated to it.

Evaluation—grading—is the keystone of education

since it determines what the children are learning, whether they are learning, and the mettle of the teacher. To mean something, it should be both continuing and consistent from day to day, from class to class. Evaluating student progress is, in most schools, the resonsibility of the teacher in spite of many who question his fitness to deduce fair and correct judgments.

Probably no other professional class is so maligned by its own members as are teachers by educational theorists, administrators, and critics. The classroom teacher has little control over the image in which he is cast by these panjandrums. Charles Jackson disparagingly writes that "one needs to spend little time in education to become familiar with the shortcomings of the teacher-dominated grading process,"[2] and Paul Allen, equally critical, believes the teacher has little confidence in himself: "When they [teachers] are placed in the role of sitting in judgment on others, they feel deeply their inadequacies and misgivings about playing such a role."[3] If, in fact, the "teacher-dominated" grading systems are filled with shortcomings, he should be dismissed. Teachers who do not feel confident of their ability to judge the work of students reveal a lack of security in their professional competence, and they would be better off doing something else.

Mr. Jackson's and Mr. Allen's conclusions, in our opinion, derive from a misinterpretation of the frustration felt by so many teachers, which, rather than from a feeling of inadequacy, often derives from administrative demands that do violence to personal convictions. Frequently, for instance, the range of grades must coincide with arbitrarily imposed percentages of high marks to low marks, known as the

Bell Curve. Students are also bound to a grade range
by their performance on standardized tests, and the
manner of recording and averaging grades, as imposed
by the administration, may receive more emphasis
than the student's achievement. An example in our
school is the required weight of the course's final examination in the student's average. Exams at the end of
every reporting period are not relevant to some subjects, and the significance placed upon them is often
unrealistic—even substantively injurious to the subject that is being taught. Take history. History is more
than dates and events. It is analysis, interpretation—a
lot else. The essay is the proper test of a student's
knowledge here. But understaffing very often makes it
unfeasible to give final examinations that are largely
comprised of essay questions (with a portion reserved
for Group 3 students who do not write essays) because
there is no time to correct them. The usual resort is the
multiple choice examination—tidbits of questions
that are unrelated and reveal not a thing about a
student's grasp of the subject and comprehension of the
whole. When the administration insists on giving the
final exam undue weight, history is distorted; it becomes a tedious exercise in memory. The weaknesses
that our illustrious critics are attributing to incompe-
tency among teachers just may be more closely related
to problems of this nature.

"Learning should be fun" and "success engenders
success" are two popular sophisms that today often
dictate the policies of education. Teachers are continually admonished to make the child happy and to
remember that his failures are the teacher's fault,
regardless of the many interacting influences on the
child's life. Grades must be correspondingly adjusted.

These young people, tomorrow's adults, will naturally expect a perpetual continuation of unmerited success. But what we all know is this: that's not the real world.

Imagine twelve school years of fun and an automatically issued diploma as their culmination! There is nothing wrong with an optimistic philosophy of life, but much harm is done to the student and to society when formal success, irrespective of achievement, is guaranteed. The student may not know his multiplication tables, nor bother to learn grammar, but he thrives on popular chiliasm. Failure is not his problem! Anyone forty years old or under reading this book will recall his own school days, which were permissive enough. But for the past two decades, any excuse at all for academic shortcomings has been accepted. Indeed, the present generation is being supplied with an abundance of alibis, fabricated for them in advance, to be capitalized upon when needed.

There can be fun in school, in a job, and in everyday life; but what we are all summarily impressed with once we get our feet wet is that much of life is spent discharging the routine, dull, but necessary chores required by our jobs or professional careers. We, as teachers, may dream of becoming twentieth-century Epictetuses. We may dream of delivering brilliant discourses, of founding great universities, of charting whole new educational worlds. But we know that for nine-tenths of us such mundane tasks as deciphering illegible handwriting and correcting atrocious grammar will be nine-tenths of our professional careers. We don't mind—if we are mature, with a perspective on the real world. The tedium prepares the rare triumph. The dedicated teacher delights in the hours actually spent with his students and feels

genuine joy when the student finally grasps an understanding of the subject. This is his highest reward. But
hours teaching are few when compared to the time
spent in preparing materials, grading work, selling
school pictures and lunch tickets, planning assembly
programs, filling out government forms, attending
meetings, handling disciplinary problems, *ad infinitum.*

No less should students be schooled in reality. Fun
should be the reward for hard work. There are courses
that are unlikely ever to be "fun" for some students;
they may nevertheless be essential for their future.
There are teachers who are less gifted than others, and
some who may stimulate certain students while getting little response from the rest of the class. If a
youngster believes that fun is an essential ingredient
of learning and, consequently, a "right," he is in for
some heartbreaking moments when his time comes to
earn a living. As well as inspiring dreams of glory,
schools should be a preparation for disaster.

Success probably does engender success, but so does
failure. We tend to forget that. Yet the annals of history
abound with men and women who rose out of poverty,
adversity, and even despair to achieve greatness for
themselves and their society. Demosthenes chewed
rocks. In his blindness, Milton viewed the broader
realms of man's existence, and though Beethoven
toward the end suffered the ironical tragedy that he
could not hear the orchestration of his own melodies,
they made sweetest hearing for the centuries. There
are creators in science, art, philosophy, and literature
who went to their graves without knowing that their
achievements would be honored and their names re-
vered; many probably died believing that they had

failed. Robert Burns' and Herman Melville's experience with the ephemeral glow of popularity left them
scarred—never to know the lasting and profound effect that their works subsequently had on the world. A
reward for achievement should be granted to students,
for they may never again receive measure for measure. But their reward should come as a result of cooperation, ability, desire, perseverance, and, above all,
self-discipline.

If we suppose that "success engenders success," then
are we to suppose that "unearned success engenders
unearned success?" We cannot continue to rear our
children in such fallacies. Education can be an invaluable first step in the realization of whatever potential
we may possess, but it cannot guarantee this. Children
first have to do their part in fully taking advantage of
those assumed invaluable benefits. But what happens
when the education they receive in public school is
itself corrupted by false values? Too many students
have found that if they do not come up to the standards
and expectations of a course or program, the standards
and expectations will come down to them. In fact,
children are little deceived. The majority are confused
by a system that provides for "crips"* and are resentful
of the high grade averages posted by their fellows in
these ersatz courses. Young people are not fooled by
euphemisms that conceal the true purpose of many
fail-safe systems that buck the student along to the
graduation platform, and they are rightfully furious
that those who have never ventured and scarcely
strived get the same leather-bound certification as
those who have given years of effort and achievement
toward that moment.

All our lives long we are graded on our performance.

A person has the *right* to have his achievement assessed; it is important to true progress. But it is also his right to be graded fairly and by a qualified authority.

The Ramseur System demands that the teacher assume the responsibility of evaluation as a vital function of his job regardless of the handicaps under which he may labor. He should continuously prepare himself to be as expert in his duties as he would expect other professionals to be in theirs. No one is perfect in judgment or knowledge, but everyone is obliged to make hard decisions. Who should be in a better position to judge student achievement than the person who is closest to the student and who is trained to do so?

The problem is, what are the criteria? All sorts of measuring bases are currently used. Tests, class participation, projects, homework, discipline, attendance, and effort—all, or several combinations of which, may serve to determine the grade of a particular student. In many schools there are as many different standards of measurement as there are people responsible for measuring. We believe that arriving at a grade, to any degree, on class participation, homework, discipline, attendance, or effort is poor practice.

Using such amorphous factors for the purpose of rating a student's actual assimilation of knowledge invites error, falsification, and injustices. Weighing merit from class participation is very subjective. The student who is reticent about speaking or who prefers to listen may possess the brightest mind in the class. A child who likes to sound off at every opportunity may be a distraction rather than an asset. Speaking up may gratify his need for expressing himself, but what the extrovert has to say may not be as pertinent as what is on the mind of a less assertive student, who may be prevented from contributing to the discussion by glib show-offs. Class participation should be encouraged as a stimulus to learning and for the practice it offers in coherent expression of thought (known in the trade as "language communication"), but it should not receive a grade unless the child has been assigned an oral report.

As for homework, who helps the student with it? Did he do it after school hours, in the afternoon or evening, or just before coming to class, when he hastily copied someone else's answers? Unfortunately, more and more students accept the practice of "sharing" assignments with other students or presenting another's work as his. Too many children today view cheating as wrong only when they are caught, and they are more likely to feel that the world has a grudge against them than shame. Assignments not done under supervision in the classroom should require the student to seek out the sources and material for a specific topic. This teaches research. He should then be tested for broadness and depth of knowledge in that subject. Such exercises, when he may confer with classmates and even borrow from their digs, will direct him in the proper channels of swapping and sharing materials, and his grade will reflect the results of his efforts. Though it may be true that amateurs invent, professionals steal, we doubt parents would approve their children being taught this in school! Under RPL, homework is graded only if it is done outside class as a part of independent study, such as research projects.

Teachers are often told to honor effort in order not to discourage a pupil who will otherwise feel that no matter what he does or how hard he tries he is destined to fail. This implies that teachers deliberately design defeat for some students. But how many men and women are paid salaries on the effort they put into a job? They are paid for what they produce, and many produce a great deal more than they are paid for. It is completely unrealistic to believe that a child who goes through school accumulating inflated grades for indifferent actual achievement will change his habits on the day of his eighteenth birthday. How many who read this book can remember pretending to have made a great effort and, with tears and stricken looks, influencing an impressionable teacher? (We pulled that one often enough ourselves.) Judging effort is totally subjective on the part of the teacher and no such evaluation should be averaged in with grades for academic achievement.

The atmosphere of an orderly classroom and the individual's attention naturally affect learning. Discipline is the *sine qua non.* Lack of discipline is both shocking and destructive to students, teachers, school, and society. Disciplinary problems will receive more attention in Chapter XIV. Here, we simply want to say that, despite the evident need for a tighter ship in our schools, a grade on any given subject should not include good conduct as a factor, because this again distorts the picture of true academic achievement. If decent behavior is to be recognized in some fashion, it should be done apart.

We view attendance with as much seriousness as behavior. Just as it matters in employment, so does it in school. The shiftless worker gets docked by his employer; the truant child penalizes himself. This is education in civic responsibility. Notoriously today, young workers arrive late to their jobs or don't show up at all.

The cost in productivity is huge; the cost to the nation in moral character that this fecklessness denotes is greater, and character—right attitudes and responsible conduct—is confirmed in our schools . . . or sometimes never. Too often, in such matters as attendance, children are indulged. Yet the appropriate penalty for a dereliction can be a lesson. If that lesson isn't learned young, it comes a lot harder later, or may never be learned at all. Yet it is common in our schools for children to be "protected" from accounting for their personal behavior. They grow into thoughtless and selfish adults with no sense of civic obligation. They become the roadside trashers of society. They must learn that if someone is absent from a job, another person must carry on the work. Consistent absenteeism places a heavier burden on the steady employees, who aren't particularly pleased. School is no different. The child who is chronically absent holds back his class and burdens the teacher with make-up work that can take twice the time lost. And few students get as much value from catching up as from their regular class time. Truancy should be handled not by trimming a child's grade, but by impressing these realities upon him. For unnecessary absences, there should be no opportunity to amend for the missed test or reading assignment.

RPL teachers grade tests, class projects, and independent studies. Every piece of work is marked according to its level. Each group is assigned special tasks; on class projects, however, all work together even though the grading takes the level at which students are studying into account. Group 3 students are not academically accountable on written expression in any subject except English. They are tested on their ability to recognize facts, relate one fact to another, and eliminate false premises. Their tests are objective, primarily multiple-choice. Their participation in projects is usually reflected through a contribution in the creative fields. Occasionally, they will express a desire to contribute, in cooperation with other members of the project group, to a written narration of the project. They are encouraged to take every opportunity to improve their self-expression. The Group 2 student will have fewer questions on his tests, but he is expected to acquire skill in writing and practice it. He must know his facts, understand them, and exercise critical analysis. Questions will require answers that vary in length from one sentence to a short paragraph. The teacher must remember that these tests are to be designed to reappraise the Group 2 student who is just entering this level and to discover the student who is ready for the demands of Group 1. The Group 1 student will be given still fewer questions, yet more difficult ones. He is expected to relate and organize facts in order to develop a theme and, by going beyond the basic material, to use divergent and convergent thinking. He will support his view with material from classroom discussions and research sources. He will be required to draw inferences in relating one body of knowledge to another. A Group 1 student will be extended primarily by essay questions. His answers must have a logical sequence; one of the most important talents to acquire is proper organization of material, which is vital to an understanding of the whole. Group 1 and 2 students will be judged on compositional skills as well as on content. They are instructed to use formal (standard) English, well-constructed sentences, correct spelling and punctuation; to avoid slang and abbreviations; and to choose appropriate expressions. Unless the value of language is stressed in all subjects, students attribute it to the idiosyncrasies of English teachers.[4] All written work is graded, and all grades are explained by the annotated corrections. Each piece of work is thoroughly checked, and comments are made to aid the student in his future endeavors. These notations may point out errors in composition or mistakes in content, praise a point well made, or suggest the need of additional information. In other words, the tests and the grading of tests should be an extension of the process of teaching and learning.

Grading systems are legion. Some schools prefer letters, others numerical symbols. Since computers are increasingly in use, the grade, regardless of how it is recorded on the report card, is converted to the numerical symbol. The scale of "A" through "F" is standard. Most teachers use a grade curve (the best paper of a given lot gets an A, whether it deserves one or not), since it allows them to prevent too great a number of failures by diplomatically adjusting fact. This is pernicious, because whereas the brighter student is accorded high marks without necessarily doing his best work, the slow student is cemented to the low or failing categories. Two students of equal ability and achievement in a given course may receive entirely different marks because they are not in the same class or they do not have the same teacher, for they will be affected by the range of talent in their particular group. The pass-fail method is more commonly used in colleges than in public schools. Research has shown that it destroys initiative.[5]

RPL was designed to eliminate as many of these

problems as possible. For each of the three groups there is a complete grading scale of A through F with the group level signified by an exponent, (A^3, B^2, C^1). Each student's work is weighed not in relation to that of the entire class (where the I.Q. range might extend from 80 to 140) but in relation to the requirements of the Group he has chosen. Because all letter grades are converted to a numerical average, numbers will frequently be used here to clarify further a student's standing, e.g. 95^3, 87^2, 73^1. In order to encourage the student continually to extend his academic reach we have substituted for an "F" in Groups 1 and 2 a "U", with the following comment on the report card to the parents:

> Joe has not failed in English 11; however, he has failed to meet the requirement for Group 1 work. I would appreciate a conference with you at your earliest convenience so that we may review his work and see how we might help him. Thank you.

A grading system that penalizes a student for attempting to do more challenging work is neither fair nor effective. Boldness—the courage to stand up to challenge—is squashed.

Just as a student is free to choose his group, he is free to choose his course grade from any of the groups in which he has worked. If, during a single semester, a student earns in the three six-weeks' (reporting) periods B^2, A^2, C^1, he may take his examination in Group 2. By this means, his performance on the exam will be averaged only with the B^2 and A^2. He may prefer to take his exam in Group 1, but this means that his grade will be averaged with the C^1. If another student earns a B^2, U^1, and B^2 and takes his exam in

Group 2, the "U" (failure to meet standards) is omitted completely when the grades are averaged. The student is thereby encouraged to try out his abilities without fear of being penalized for his gallant attempt.

Many schools run on the semester system in which each subject is completed (passed or failed) in a ninety school-day period (South Carolina requires a school year to be a hundred and eighty days of actual teaching). Under this division, RPL allows the student four chances to change his group every semester. He has made the initial choice at the beginning of the course after taking sample tests; he may choose again after a 4½ week period; at the end of the first nine-week period; and before the mid-semester exams. At the end of 13½ weeks, he is allowed his fourth and final choice. Grades for these periods will be averaged as they are for a six-week reporting period. The mean is calculated within separate groups. There is no attempt to mix grades from different groups, because this would be misleading as to the skills acquired.

The following illustrations are taken from the files of our students. These, reduced in size, are the grade sheets we used when the school was on a six-weeks' reporting period. (Later, a copy of the semester grade sheet will be shown.) They should clarify the flexibility of the RPL grading system, the opportunities it offers students, and the educational values that are built into it.

The first example is Joe Spitzler, (Figure 1) who failed to do well on the sample Group 1 and 2 test (10 and 12). His spelling, punctuation, and sentence structure were very poor. His Group 3 grade was a low passing mark (72). As a result of these orientation

Figure 1

SUBJECT World History	YEAR _____
STUDENT'S NAME Spitzler, Joe	GROUP I 10
SUBJECT TEACHER N. Smith	GROUP II 12
HOMEROOM TEACHER S. Carter	GROUP III 72

	Grade		Group
1st 6 weeks			
Comments	87	B	3
2nd 6 weeks			
Comments	91	B	3
3rd 6 weeks			
Comments	96	A	3
1st Sem. Exam.	98		3
1st Sem. Average	92		3
4th 6 weeks			
Comments	43	U	2
5th 6 weeks			
Comments	35	U	2
6th 6 weeks			
Comments	98	A	3
2nd Sem. Exam.	95		3
2nd Sem. Average	97		3

Pilot Light Form 2 Year   Grade 93   Group 3

tests and counsel with his teacher, he chose Group 3 for the first period. Although Joe had difficulty reading and had turned down the offer to take an oral test given to students who reading handicaps are severe enough to make even the most simply worded quiz impossible for them to understand, he made an 87^3 average. (See *Grade,* 1st 6 weeks). The delight Joe felt over this accomplishment encouraged him to do even better. His second and third reporting periods showed a steady rise to an "A", and his semester exam (98^3) gave him an average for the semester of 92^3. (All figures are rounded out to the next whole number.) At the conference with his teacher prior to the beginning of the fourth reporting period, Joe expressed a desire, ignited by his success, to try Group 2. A review of his sample tests did not prognosticate a very successful venture into the higher level because his problems in writing were serious. He had, however, the right to make the attempt, and he did not have to fear the grade, since he had already assured his standing for the year in his group. *Joe was investing his previously earned capital in a try at something new.*

As shown in Figure 1, Joe's difficulties in reading and writing prevented him from succeeding in Group 2 (43^2), but he persisted through the fifth reporting period (35^2). He then returned to Group 3 and finished the year at that level. The 43^2 and 35^2 were eliminated from his final average. Joe's comment at the end of the year was, "I couldn't make that Group 2, but at least I know now I'm not a dummy."

There is more to the story. After Joe's mother called the school to express her delight over his progress and his resulting self-respect, the teacher reviewed his cumulative folder and found the following information. Joe entered the first grade at the age of 7. He was in a homogeneously grouped system through the ninth grade and was placed, all nine years, in the section for very low achievers. He came to us already handicapped. For half of his schooling he had been socially promoted. His I.Q. was rated as 89, which the Ramseur System proved was nonsense. After completing high school, he entered the U.S. Army, where he received two citations, the Commendation Medal, and the Soldier's Medal. At the time of this writing, he is operating a small and very successful business.

Donald Benson has remained in Group 3 for five reporting periods (Figure 2) and tells his teacher that he wishes to try Group 2 for the last period. He will not be allowed to make the transfer because he has failed to file the request earlier and, therefore, will not have been in Group 2 for the required two periods. Before this limitation was placed on a student's options, some chose to move to a higher or lower group for the last stretch in order to preserve the grade average they had compiled during the balance of the year. This dodge permitted them to avoid work the final six weeks without fear of having their attack of spring fever reflected on the final report card.

Bill Dodson (Figure 3), who is a good Group 2 student with a 92^2 average, has an automobile accident that keeps him out of school for a full reporting period. When he finds that his injury will not allow him to do the work necessary to keep up with Group 2, he is advised to switch to Group 3 and take the tests in that category in order to avoid too heavy a load. At the beginning of the next reporting period, when he returns to school, he has the opportunity to go back to Group 2 or, if he finds this level still too difficult be-

Figure 2

SUBJECT	English III	YEAR	
STUDENT'S NAME	Benson, Donald	GROUP I	41
SUBJECT TEACHER	M. Little	GROUP II	60
HOMEROOM TEACHER	T. Jones	GROUP III	83

		Grade		Group
1st 6 weeks				
Comments		85	C	3
2nd 6 weeks				
Comments		92	B	3
3rd 6 weeks				
Comments		87	B	3
	1st Sem. Exam.	83		3
	1st Sem. Average	87		3
4th 6 weeks				
Comments		94	B	3
5th 6 weeks				
Comments		88	B	3
6th 6 weeks				
Comments				
	2nd Sem. Exam.			
	2nd Sem. Average			

Pilot Light Form 2 Year   Grade _____ Group _____

Figure 3

SUBJECT	Psychology		YEAR	
STUDENT'S NAME	Dodson, Bill		GROUP I	70
SUBJECT TEACHER	J. Stuart		GROUP II	82
HOMEROOM TEACHER	L. Green		GROUP III	99

		Grade	Group
1st 6 weeks			
Comments		85	C	2

I think I can do Group 2 and I need to improve my writing skills.

		Grade	Group
2nd 6 weeks			
Comments		90	B	2

I wish to remain. This is getting easier.

		Grade	Group
3rd 6 weeks			
Comments		94	A	2
	1st Sem. Exam.	98		2
	1st Sem. Average	91		2

Same choice.

		Grade	Group
4th 6 weeks			
Comments				3

Bill will be out much of this period because of an automobile accident and will not be able to do some of the Group 2 assignments. He will return to Group 2 later.

J. Stuart

		Grade	Group
5th 6 weeks			
Comments				

		Grade	Group
6th 6 weeks			
Comments				
	2nd Sem. Exam.			
	2nd Sem. Average			

Pilot Light Form 2 Year   Grade _____   Group _____ cause of long absence, to remain where he is and receive credit for the entire course at Group 3 level. The reason for his decision is recorded on the grade sheet, and he may request that a copy of that sheet be sent with his other records to the college of his choice so that he will not be deprecated for an unavoidable event that could have prevented him from completing the course successfully.

RPL takes class participation, homework, discipline, attendance, and effort into consideration in a different manner. We do not grade these intangibles, but all are ultimately reflected in a student's performance. Class participation, for example, despite the reservations we noted earlier, is a positive good. It helps students reinforce what has been learned from lectures, projects, and tests. Children hear viewpoints other than their own. This broadens their understanding and cultivates tolerance. RPL training of teachers (Chapter IV) encourages a maximum of active participation by students, who are not over-awed and do not fear they will be cut down. Homework is another tool extensively used by RPL. A student who studies on his own time is learning more about the subject, and what he learns in this manner makes the understanding of class work easier and more enjoyable. If he has faithfully completed his outside assignments, this will be reflected in tests, projects, and so forth. As for discipline, only incorrigibles fail to respond to the fairness of the Ramseur System. What complaints can a student have to excuse bad behavior? He cannot claim discrimination of any kind, since he himself chooses the level he feels best suited to him. His work is on file, annotated and graded: he can go over it whenever he wishes, or take it to someone else for review should he feel that he has been treated unfairly. The slow or culturally and economically less fortunate child is never set apart from his classmates; he isn't deprived of the stimulus of quick minds or a window into different backgrounds, ways and values. His "self-concept" won't be damaged, either, since he is never pointed out as a member of any specific group nor forced to compete at a level with which he can't contend. If a slow student suddenly "blooms," he can take advantage of it almost at once—he is not held back, panting at the bit, for administrative reasons. Similarly, the exceptionally gifted child has no cause to harbor a slow burn against those of his classmates who are less luckily endowed. He is never held back. He gets the high grades his work deserves, and the integrity of those grades is preserved. Instead of resentment, compassion is the more likely reaction; and if the bright child of comfortable background possesses any generosity of spirit, he may come to respect human values that have nothing to do with money or the intellectual faculties. Practically every human being has a grace or gift of some kind. The Ramseur System not only reduces obstructions to tolerance; it nurtures tolerance.

Since there are no reasonable grounds for complaint, it is obvious that the child who persists in offensive conduct does so gratuitously and inexcusably. We will deal at length with disciplinary problems later, as we've promised; meantime, it suffices to note that under RPL no alibis remain to the unruly child, who, thanks to the unimpeachable fairness of the system, is often a minority of one instead of a gang of three or four, and as such is much more easily handled. The malcontent is scorned by the other children, which has a great moderating effect.

Not every child can be guaranteed academic laurels. A person may put forth a great deal of effort in order to learn to sing or play an instrument, yet may not be blessed with the talent. A boy may dream of running a hundred yards for the winning touchdown, and practice sprints for hours, only to discover he lacks the speed, size, and strength to play competitive football. Everyone needs dreams. Some will be realized, others will not. The individual must himself strive to fulfill his aspirations; they cannot be handed to him on a platter. RPL encourages dreams; it is sympathetic with a child's highest aspirations; but it focuses them within the realm of the possible. Though under RPL he is not permitted for long to indulge in the fantastic, with an inflated notion of his ratiocinative capacities, a sincere effort on his part will help him to realize his full potential and measure his accomplishment. There is no need for social promotion or debased academic standards to meet an average.

We've been asked by some fellow educators, "What you really have is just a grading system, isn't it?" This is a misconception of the first order. The criteria and techniques that we use in grading arise from the interior structure of the Ramseur System, of which the ability to make an honest assessment of oneself and others is a vital component. The need to judge and be judged is basic to man. We must all learn to distinguish good from bad, the false from the real. We must all measure ourselves and those with whom we deal in life. Realistic evaluation is the foundation of choice; man is the only creature endowed with free choice and, by virtue of which, a degree of autonomous direction in his existence. It is important that he exercise his choices with both feet on the ground if he is to preserve this control. Under RPL, the grading system is an integral part of the entire curriculum of the school (to be discussed) and cannot be isolated from the whole. Evaluation under this system is the end that the means and methods must justify.

An official of a large company was concerned that his son had a B^2 while a classmate had an A^3, when everyone knew that the friend was not a good student. We were asked to explain the apparent wrong. This is the parallel we drew for him.

We penciled three lines on a sheet of paper.

——————————— ——————————— ———————————

We asked the father whether these three lines would serve to describe the division of his company in the following manner.

(Executive Branch   (Operations,   (Labor, skilled &
                     Scientists)   non-skilled)

——————————— ——————————— ———————————

He agreed. We then asked whether he was the top executive of his company? No. But was he an executive? Yes. Did he make the same salary as his chief? No. Would the salaries go like this?

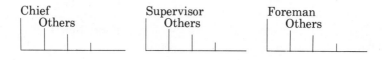

The answer, "Yes."

In other words, in each branch there was a hierarchy of positions and commensurate salaries. Finally, we asked him to change the heading of the branches of his company to Groups 1, 2, and 3 and consider the grade range comparable to the salary range.

Group 1	Group 2	Group 3

He was reminded that in the world of business there would be only one chief (A[1]) but in this system there could be many. Grading, therefore, is a necessary part of education, but it should be accurate in presentation, fair to the student, and revealing to the teacher.

Footnotes, Chapter V

*"Crip" courses are those designed to assure a passing grade to students. These courses are easy, require very little work, and are dubbed by students as "crips."

[1] Miss Becky Milling was the first teacher to put Pilot Light into practice in grade levels below secondary education. She left South Carolina to teach in her home state but since has returned to Camden and is teaching in the Lugoff-Elgin Elementary school. She has, also, changed her name—Mrs. R. Eric Brown—and she, her husband, and small daughter live in Camden.

[2] Charles D. Jackson, "Students Grade Themselves," *Today's Education,* LIX (October, 1970), p. 25.

[3] Paul M. Allen, "The Student Evaluation Dilemma," *Today's Education,* LVII (February, 1969), p. 50.

[4] Henry W. Bragdon, "Neglected Resource: The Essay Question," *Teaching the Social Studies,* edited by Richard E. Gross, Walter E. McPhie, and Jack R. Fraenkel, (Scranton, Pennsylvania: International Textbook Company, 1969), p. 493.

[5] J. N. Hook, *The Teaching of High School English,* (New York: Ronald Press Company, 1965), pp. 74-75.

Chapter VI
Evaluation: Credit Where Credit Is Due

Examples of misrepresentation of a student's academic standing in relation to his fellow classmates • Grade inflation • The steps of classifying a student's class rank under RPL • RPL student records • Involvement of the student in his academic profile • Identifying competency

Stan, a rising senior, is worried. Bright and conscientious, he has taken a full schedule of college preparatory courses—genetics, philosophy, trigonometry, advanced placement history, and English numbered among them—subjects in which 99 averages are rare. Now he discovers that, in spite of having the third highest PSAT score in his class, he will not be recommended by the school for a scholarship because his cumulative average (86) does not rank him as one of the top ten students. Why? How come? Well, because —as so often happens—the school compares averages irrespective of the relative difficulty of the courses. Some are college preparatory, others not. It's easier to get an A in General Math than a B in calculus.

Sylvia is 18 and a senior. Her I.Q. is recorded as 92, and she is 50 percentile and *below* in all categories on her achievement test scores. She has, nevertheless, the highest average in most of her classes and is elected to the school's honor society. There is nothing on her records to show that the subjects in which she has earned her grades are designed for slow learners. She may, therefore, outrank Stan in their class.

Ranking students is the placing of them on a scale based on the cumulative academic averages. Some institutions of higher learning will accept only those among the top ten percent. Colleges and universities need a clear and accurate accounting in order to select applicants from public schools fairly. They want to know the potential of these students. Are they scholastically prepared for the work expected of them at a higher level? Secondary schools must furnish this information. Ranking students is, consequently, whether we like it or not, necessary.

There are many different methods resorted to, such as weighing courses according to their application to college requirements, "tracking" students and defining those in the college preparatory track as acceptable candidates, and taking the class averages of all students and placing them correspondingly.

Ranking is one of the most difficult tasks of the school administration, and it can ruffle more parental feathers than failing to name someone's darling in the local newspaper as an extra in "The King and I." Each method has its flaws, and all tend to contradict other goals. For instance, weighing courses for values does not help to define the relative strengths and weaknesses of teachers who conduct different classes of that same course. Some teachers are more demanding than others; and any computation of rank from student averages in weighted courses is, besides, difficult without access to computers. Tracking, as we've noted, stigmatizes the poorer students and fosters discrimination, while ranking by yearly averages irrespective of what is studied is neither fair nor realistic, because students with a shallow sense of values—often, sadly, implanted by their parents—sign up for snap courses, avoiding those tough subjects that they need to master if they are truly to be prepared for college.

The consequences has been the universally deplored phenomenon of grade inflation. An editorial in a southwestern metropolitan newspaper recently lamented:

—The evidence continues to grow that there is a serious slippage in the quality of public education nationally. The impact is being noted in the employment market place.

—Personnel directors are being warned by research studies that grade-point averages should be viewed skeptically as predictors of job success because of "grade inflation" in the schools and colleges.

—There is a paradox; more students are receiving higher grades while national test scores are declining sharply. For example, during this decade standardized test scores have fallen significantly while at the University of Chicago 30 per cent of the students have honor grades compared to 19 per cent in 1967 . . . [1]

Such complaints pop up ubiquitously in the press. William Raspberry, the eminent black columnist, and Jesse Jackson, the apostle of black self-help, have indignantly attacked meaningless grades and the degradation of educational requirements. Reverend Jackson, criticizing teachers who pass failing students or misrepresent their achievement (and, thus, cripple them), has said, "That's not liberal. This is neglect, and neglect is close to hate."[2] *Time* quotes Harvard's Riesman, "The only places in schools today where people are really encouraged to perform up to capacity are in sports and the band ... elitism is almost as dirty a word as sexism or racism."[3] The American public, white and black, is alarmed by the sorry state of education, which is now manifest in the uneven performance of young people at their jobs. Their education is responsible and must account for it. Public schools must respond to the rising demand for quality and a fair, accurate ranking system that enables institutions of higher learning to select truly qualified students. Colleges and universities, in turn, must provide business and industry with a realistic determination of student achievement—which inflated grades do not.

The RPL ranking system fairly places students in their true class standing. It is designed to complement any other system of grading and to work in a school operating under more than one. Since class position is required only for colleges and universities, two main objectives were considered when RPL ranking was planned: (1) to find a simpler and more effective system than those now available; (2) to design one that would not penalize the student for challenging himself in some of the more difficult background courses. Classifying students under the RPL method includes three steps.

1. Courses are categorized as academic and non-academic (in accordance with the terms defined in South Carolina by the South Carolina Department of Education). Non-academic courses do not figure in class rank. Academic courses receive one point for identification.

2. The academic point "1" is then multiplied inversely by the group points. Group points are given for the level at which the student works. Group 1 receives

three group points for the accelerated program requiring additional skills, and Group 2 receives two points for average and above average work within a course (also college preparatory). Group 3 receives one point for an understanding of the subject, with no requirements for the student to demonstrate his knowledge through means that he does not possess and that could prevent him from showing what he *is* able to do. This last group represents competency but not college preparatory level.

> Example: One academic point (AP) times three group points (GP) for Group 1 level work equals three rank points (RP).
>
> $$AP \times GP = RP$$
> $$1 \times 3 \ = \ 3$$

3. The final step involves the grade average. No student with a high grade average in a low group level can outrank another student making a low grade average in a higher group level. Students are first compared by the number of rank points they have earned. Bill, Jim, and Bob have acquired, respectively, 50, 50, and 47 rank points. Bill and Jim appear to be equal, but here is where grades are used to distinguish further between students.

In earning their 50 rank points each over four years of high school, Bill averaged an 85, but Jim averaged 85.8; therefore, Jim will place higher than Bill in the final analysis. The third student, Bob, has an academic average for four years of 90; however, he did not take some courses in a higher level and as a consequence has earned only 47 *rank* points. The 90 average with fewer rank points cannot outrank a lower grade earned in more demanding work. This, therefore, is how they stand:

> Jim—50 rank points—grade average 85.8
> Bill—50 rank points—grade average 85
> Bob—47 rank points—grade average 90

Besides providing an academic profile that is fairer and more accurate, and one that is stripped of such irrelevancies as pats on the back for effort or good attendance, RPL's records, which include the student's folder and grade sheets, give invaluable additional information. Every class has a filing cabinet with a folder for each student. The folders contain the child's work in the order it was assigned, and they are used in the following ways: (1) The student may wish to go over his file in order to check his own progress. (Has he repeated mistakes, made new ones, or shown steady improvement?) *He is able to determine his weaknesses, define his problems, and concentrate on eliminating them.* (2) The folder is an up-to-the-minute record from which the parent can gauge not only how his child is getting along but also *how intelligent are the assignments and their grading by his instructor.* (Nothing can be swept under the rug.) (3) Teachers use the folders to study student weaknesses and strengths in designing more effective tests or concentrating more on work to which the student has responded with interest and progress. (4) The folder is an important aid for counseling at the beginning of a reporting period. The contents give the teacher a brief review of the student's performance, a mnemonic refresher that is most helpful when advising any child on whether he should attempt the next step in the program.

The grade sheet, in conjunction with the folder, at a glance gives a cumulative graph of the student's condition. A review of his comments coupled with his actual performance can be used analytically by himself and his teacher. The grades and his upward mobility (or lack of same) help the child come to terms with himself. We taught a young man at Camden High School whom we'll call Bob Smith. Bob started the school year in Group 1. His comments at the end of each marking period, when he made his choise as to which study Group to pursue, illustrate the self-portrait that a student is allowed to draw. As shown in Figure 4, Bob did poorly on all his sample tests. Nevertheless, he chose the most difficult level of work. At the end of the school year, after scanning his evaluation sheet, Bob burst forth with a candid appraisal of how he was doing, saying to us, "Wow, that doesn't look too pretty. Guess I can't fool anybody with this." He was right.

Sally Fry (Figure 5) was another student altogether. There are no comments on Sally's grade sheet. A student is not required to comment; failure to do so, however, leaves final judgment of Sally as a student to anyone who reviews the grade sheet. She set out in Group 2 and was content to stay there, posting good marks. Why didn't she have a fling with Group 1 in biology, where she would have deepened her knowledge: The college entrance examination board may wonder whether she lacks a challenging spirit or whether she wasn't mentally lazy. Maybe her decision to stick with Group 2 is explainable without engendering questions about her fitness for college; such as, for example, a heavy schedule in other Group 1 classes that she was taking at the time; but who knows, when Sally herself offers no clues? Fact is, Sally had to work

Figure 4

SUBJECT ___United States History___   YEAR _____

STUDENT'S NAME ___Smith, Bob___   GROUP I ___20___

SUBJECT TEACHER ___L. Bell___   GROUP II ___23___

HOMEROOM TEACHER ___R. Brown___   GROUP III ___50___

1st 6 weeks		Grade		Group
Comments		20	U	I

I wish to start in Group I—no problem.

2nd 6 weeks				
Comments		32	F	3

I might as well do Group 3—Colleges don't pay
attention to anything but grades. They don't care
where you get them.

3rd 6 weeks				
Comments		30	U	2
	1st Sem. Exam.	30		3
	1st Sem. Average	31		3

Guess I had better try Group 2.
Group 3 is too easy and I need
to have a challenge.

4th 6 weeks				
Comments		15	U	2

O.K. It's about time I settle down. I'm going to Group
2 for the rest of the year.

5th 6 weeks				
Comments		15	U	1

I can do the work. I just hate history. My sixth grade
teacher was a horror, and she made me hate history.
Put me in Group I.

6th 6 weeks				
Comments		50	F	3
	2nd Sem. Exam.	25		3
	2nd Sem. Average	37		3

If I do extra good on this period
and also on the exam, will I get
credit for the year?

Pilot Light Form 2 Year   Grade ___33___   Group ___3___

Figure 5

SUBJECT ___Biology I_____ YEAR _____
STUDENT'S NAME ___Fry, Sally_____ GROUP I ___67___
SUBJECT TEACHER ___B. Carlyle_____ GROUP II ___80___
HOMEROOM TEACHER ___V. Clarke_____ GROUP III ___100__

1st 6 weeks		Grade		Group
Comments		85	C	2

2nd 6 weeks				
Comments		92	B	2

3rd 6 weeks				
Comments		94	B	2
	1st Sem. Exam.	91		2
	1st Sem. Average	91		2

4th 6 weeks				
Comments		96	A	2

5th 6 weeks				
Comments		94	B	2

6th 6 weeks				
Comments		97	A	2
	2nd Sem. Exam.	96		2
	2nd Sem. Average	96		2

Pilot Light Form 2 Year   Grade ___94___ Group ___2___ hard just to maintain her grades in Biology Group 2—she realized she was not ready to assume an additional load. But to avoid false assumptions by third parties, students are encouraged to express their reasons for what they decide to do. If the instructor is aware of a student's problems, he may make a note on the grade sheet—though teachers have been asked to refrain from subjective forays whenever possible.

The permanent record is composed of the student transcript, recorded standardized tests scores, class rank, and pertinent information about the student's health. Since an exponent accompanying a grade (80^2) is not unusual, all RPL students' permanent records have a letter attached explaining the RPL grouping and grading system (Figure 6). The letter protects the student by explaining the emphasis placed on level of work rather than on grades alone.

Fig. 6.

Dear Parent:

Your child, _____, is involved in a method of education known as RPL. A brief explanation of the system will be furnished here, and additional information will be given by the teachers in the different subject fields upon request.

RPL is a method of education designed to individualize instruction, i.e., to meet the needs of each student based upon his capabilities, problems, talents, and future plans. The student will be exposed to all levels of a given course and will be free to choose the level in which he will work.

The three levels are the following: Group 1 is a highly accelerated level, requiring the exercise of writing skills and the higher level of learning skills. The students in this group are given the opportunity to move ahead in their work and to be involved in independent study.

Group 2 requires a good foundation in grammar, and the student in this group is trained to write for the different subject fields and to exercise learning skills above the basic skill of recall. The skills of this group are basic to success in Group 1.

Groups 1 and 2 are college preparatory. Group 3, a non-college preparatory group, does not require the skills of writing.

All class work is designed to involve all students; therefore, no student is pointed out through classroom projects or assignments as belonging to any given group. Equal participation in the class is granted and encouraged. The difference in the work required is reflected in the reading assignments, independent study, research and tests. No student is bound to one group. He may change after each reporting period (report card due date) as his own desire and capabilities dictate. Since he is exposed at all times to three levels, he is prepared to recognize the time to move to another group. To acquire a course evaluation, he must be in a group for two reporting periods and complete the course requirements for that group. Groups are never averaged together as each group reflects the acquisition of different and/or additional skills.

The evaluation (grade) of the student's work carries with it an exponent to designate the level in which the grade is earned. (B^2) Each group has a grade range of A through D. Failure to meet the required standards in Groups 2 and 1 will earn a U. This is a warning grade. If, however, the student persists in working in a group in which he has U's and earns no passing grade, then the U must, at the completion of the course, become an F. If a Group 3 student fails to acquire the passing mark, he will receive an F. Special problems will be decided after a conference with the parents, teachers, and school counselors.

All RPL students have a file on their work, with the teacher's evaluation clearly explained. Students are encouraged to study these analyses of their work and to use these evaluations as an aid to improvement. Also, students are encouraged to take their files home for parent review. In this way the parent can have an up-to-date evaluation of the child's work, and a better understanding of the goals and accomplishments in each subject course.

A copy of this letter will be attached to the first report card issued by an RPL teacher. The teacher would appreciate the parents' signatures to show that they have read the letter and are aware of the subjects in which their child is working under RPL.

We, the RPL teachers, look forward to working with your child and appreciate your cooperation and interest in preparing him for the future. We hope that you will feel free to seek any information on or evaluation of your child's progress.

Sincerely,

_____

Teacher

_____

Subject

_____

Parent's signature

**In my course I have elected to eliminate the first graded papers in the final average if the student's work shows improvement for the rest of the course. I am considering his first period as a training exercise so that the students may become familiar with the system and my style of teaching and grading. To have the grade eliminated the student must not acquire a lower mark in that group for the duration of the course. No grade, other than the first one, will be eliminated.

Thus, the student is involved in all phases of his academic profile. He, by his free choice of group, judges his potential, grades his own effort, decides what his goals are, and accomplishes as much as he chooses within them. He decides against what standards he wishes to compete. He is aware of the different requirements and what each group is tested on. Because he is exposed to the materials of every level, he is able to pace himself in relation to students of all ranges of intellect. This exposure helps him to assess his capacity more accurately, and since he has no fear of misplacement, unfair categorization, or being docked for an ambitious leap forward that maybe failed, grades are less threatening. He can exercise some control of them. His records do not become a restricted file that is scrutinized only by figures of authority, whom he imagines as hooded executioners in some medieval torture chamber.

What about the other end of the educational pole—competency level? The shocking revelation of the alarming number of chronically deficient graduates who are being churned out of public high schools has kicked off a race by educators to fleece more fat funding from the public treasury for studies of causes and cures. What a windfall this has been for political and academic paperpushers! Everybody gets a committee to lead. The committees breed other committees, and these superfetate into still more committees. Committees must be established to regulate the previously approved committees. And, naturally, there will have to be committees to review the situation, if one can still locate it, and committees to study the findings of that committee—and on and on until the student is quite forgotten in the bureaucratic labyrinth. Oh, and let's not forget the workshops that every committee will spawn.

Forgive us if we sound like veterans of a thousand battles. We are. And what we can tell the taxpaying parent is, RPL dispenses with the excuse for one more raid on his pocketbook. We did not design RPL with competency level in mind—proficiency in the rudimentary skills of reading, writing, and arithmetic is assured because of the design. *Competency is the definition of Group 3.*

A student should have one rank point for each course he has taken if he has passed his course in Group 3. What about Joe Spitzler—the boy who made A's in Group 3 but could not write a simple, coherent sentence? If Joe has been taught under the Ramseur System throughout his schooling, he probably would never have found himself that far without being able to write. When Joe came to us he could read the test questions in world history and was able to express himself orally—showing that he knew his lessons in that particular subject—but he was a disaster in his English class. Group 3, remember, in English, requires basic writing. Under RPL, a student can be detected as below standard the moment he doesn't perform on that primary level. Right away, he can be helped, and before it's too late. Under RPL, a student (on a 18-unit credit basis) is, by gum, functional if he has 18 rank points at the end of high school education.

Some states are now insisting on a standardized competency test. If an RPL student has passed his Group 3 courses and then fails to satisfy requirements in any part of such a test, his school records should be checked. Everything is there. Nothing is hidden. There are no freebies in the grades. If the work record confirms that he is competent, then *the validity of the standardized test must be re-examined.* We don't mean to suggest that such tests are always structurally questionable, but there are often subjective factors that aren't taken into account. Did Sally Teyham "freeze" when confronted with an examination of such importance? Was it just a bad day? If, on the other hand, from reviewing her file, it's found that Sally was not given the necessary work, then her teacher needs to do some explaining. RPL is not proof against weak or softhearted teachers; but the RPL records will discover them.

Some students, because of inherent incapacity, will not become literate under any system. We can no longer afford to ignore this reality. We must, however, diagnose such cases early in order to provide for them.

Group 4 is where the academically handicapped child can receive special care.

Since Group 4 has no points, the student will have only a unit credit for the completion of the course at that level.

$$1 \text{ AP} \times \text{GP} = \text{RP}$$
$$1 \times \ \ 0 = \ \ 0$$

We caution the teacher against using the exponent 4 (80^4) except in special circumstances, such as those unfortunate children with that Gordion knot of physiological and psycho-emotional problems known as "learning disabilities," which can totally obstruct their ability to absorb (some may have high IQs) even though they are cooperative and willing to do their best. The 4 must not be used to pass a disruptive, rude, or lazy student who gives nothing to his education and, obviously, gets nothing out of it. He must comprehend one thing—to get anywhere, we all have to work.

Or so most of us believe, even as the public wonders at the increasing number of college freshmen who matriculate untaught and unprepared. College and university officials are the first to scream about lax secondary school standards—while they themselves continue dishing out higher grades.

One cannot help puzzling over this contradiction. Many parents are now sending their children to summer camps sponsored by colleges, where, at a price, they are supposedly taught those things they did not learn in grammar and high schools. If indeed the colleges can accomplish the feat of drumming into young people in six weeks or so what they apparently spent the first twelve years of their education shutting out of their minds, they should share their secret with public schools across the land. This would help parents save every dollar possible to allay the exorbitant cost of higher education, because these special remedial camps don't come free. We are dubious. But the demand that something be done to teach the high school graduate basic reading, writing, and arithmetic has brought forth an avalanche of studies, testings, seminars, and workshops—*ad infinitum*—of the fruitless kind we've alluded to earlier. President Carter is asking for $12.9 *billion* dollars (the biggest increase in education since L.B. Johnson's administration) to support these exercises in futility.

Indeed, there is an almost endless list of quack cures for the ills of academe, and if they continue to be as successful as the ones we've seen, education will only become worse while the cost mounts. Why not use the Ramseur System? We've tested it for fifteen years. It works. By incorporating it into high school programs across the country, it will reduce that flood of unqualified students who swamp the admissions offices of universities.

Furthermore, under RPL, blame for illiteracy falls squarely where it belongs—on the student himself or his teacher—with records to back it up. As for the incompetent young person, or the young man or woman suffering from what may be incurable intellectual sloth, neither of whom should be directed toward college, the RPL system finds that child out without the need of new government interventions that will clutter the academic bureaucracy, which is top heavy enough already. And, we don't mind adding, without the crocodile tears and demagogic exhortations of politicians who support any program, regardless of cost, to save the wee kiddies of this country. And, listen—all it requires is an understanding of the system. RPL has been humming along these fifteen years without a dime's aid from anyone. We pass it on to you the same way, FREE!

Footnotes, Chapter VI

[1]"Quality of Education," *The State,* Editorial, March 18, 1976.
[2]Alex Poinsett, "Push For Excellence," *Ebony,* February, 1977. p. 109.
[3]"High Schools Under Fire," *Time,* November 14, 1977.

Chapter **VII**
Foundation of Success: The Library

*Examples of poor use of the library • The RPL
teacher, librarian and students*

Having tested the students in her grammar class, Mrs.
Grimball writes individual prescriptions and prepares
the drills that each pupil needs. After a few weeks of
prescribing for, reexamining, and reviewing twenty-
two students who represent about twenty-two levels of
capacity, the harried Mrs. Grimball hits upon a way
of maintaining her sanity and keeping the long queue
of problem-children still waiting for her guidance from
tearing the walls down. Each day she allows a number
of them to go to the library to browse. After all, the best
way to appreciate effective use of language is through
great literary works, isn't it? Sure, go to it. With such
vague instructions, her students spend most of their
bibliophilic hours enjoying the companionship of
friends, tearing pictures out of magazines and books,
or decorating them with imperishable art. While Mrs.
Grimball is salvaging her nerves, the librarians are
slowly losing theirs.

"A student deprived of good library service is a student deprived of a good education."[1] Granted, but the
availability of pencils doesn't necessarily teach a child
how to write. The purpose of a literary program is not
only to put the right book into the hands of the right

child at the right time, but to help the classroom teacher use the right educational tool at the right time. To this end, a good high school library should keep an ever-growing quantity of valuable educational aids readily available to teachers and students alike. This only rarely happens.

Timmy has to write a term paper on the left eyeball of the common housefly for his biology teacher, Mr. Horace Adams Eggleston, who always signs his full name and tacks on Ph.D. at the end. That Timmy is a slow reader and can barely compose a declaratory sentence does not excuse him: all the students in Mr. Eggleston's class *have to write* a term paper on the eyeball of the housefly—the common housefly, that is. After all, he has to preserve his reputation as a "stiff" teacher. He's proud of it. It's no skin off his hornbill nose that a throng of students must use the same materials at the same time; as a matter of fact, he hasn't bothered to determine what materials are available. He hasn't even told his students how to write a paper in biology. Why should he? That is the job of the English teacher. So, Timmy carefully copies every word, comma, and period out of some encyclopedia and any other source the long-suffering librarian can dig up for him. He at least learns how to *copy*—plagiarism, it's called, though Timmy does not know this. Miss Lily, the librarian, cannot decide which of Mr. Eggleston's research assignments is the more exasperating—this, or the previous one on the modest subject of mental health. But she sighs, consoling herself. Maybe this is how Edward Gibbon got started on *The Decline and Fall of the Roman Empire*.

Sammy, who was assigned a paper on George Washington—date of birth, place of birth, father and mother, education, etc.—worked hard to fulfill the requirements that were neatly typed on his low-level "contract sheet." He spent hours. He searched through the stacks like a lost soul. Finally, in desperation, he asked Miss Lily to help him, because he couldn't dig out the facts. She gently steered him from Washington *State* to a short biography of that big, stern-faced fellow in a white wig.

Teachers under RPL provide guidance that eliminates this kind of foolishness. They demand of each student only what he can handle in order to accomplish the requirements for his chosen level of work. The research they assign is always both practical and feasible.

Any student, regardless of ability or diligence, can benefit from the offerings of the library. But few will unless they are directed to sources that serve their particular needs. Selection is important—and it's not easy! You don't refer a thirteen-year-old who suffers from arthritis of the tongue to *The Quintessential Dictionary.* You don't simply let loose a seventeen-year-old with a 90 IQ on Dorland's *Illustrated Medical Dictionary* and ask him to write up a paper on glossological phlogosis. Reference books and other materials that are stocked in high school libraries must be selected for widely varying capacities of comprehension. They should be interesting as well as informative, and they should fully answer what the student has been asked to look up. The limits must be set by the RPL teacher (assignments have to be explicit, the topics carefully structured) in accordance with a student's particular goals and the objectives of his group; teacher and student collaborate on any library project to the end that the student is able to do creditably. At this point, the librarian becomes indispensable.

Remember two things. RPL group projects are assigned at the *beginning* of each course. They are comprehensive, and students are informed how the projects can be carried from one level to another. A Group 3 requirement, for example, must be included in a Group 2 work assignment. Both Group 3 and Group 2 work are included in a Group 1 project. This often motivates a student to try the stiffer challenge. He doesn't have to start all over on a new project—a prospect that would discourage many otherwise ambitious children.

During the first reporting period the RPL instructor consults with each student about the project he prefers. Naturally, it is helpful to find a subject in which the child has an inherent interest, which will make his work more exciting; but the topic settled on must be pertinent to the *course*—not just a pro forma exercise to satisfy a credit. Too often, content is sacrificed on the altar of juvenile interest, whereas what the child needs to learn is that he must broaden his horizon of knowledge. This is sometimes best accomplished by an assignment that forces him to venture into what he may discover to be intriguing fields.

Next, a list of the students and their project topics is taken by the teacher to the librarian. Togther they determine whether (1) there is sufficient material on the subjects chosen by the pupils, and whether (2) there is apporpriate material on hand for the three groups. At this point, the instructor restricts the topics (no broad subjects on mental health, world cooperation, or modern economic trends) so that they can be dealt with by students in the time allotted.

Once the topics are cut to size, a list of them with the students' names and their group goes to the librarian. This helps her pilot each child to the materials he can handle. By being forewarned, she has been able to pull out of the stacks what each group is going to need, saving her time and energy. She is able to plan intelligently ahead, and she takes pleasure in the new respect for her domain that properly prepared students show. In fact, she glows in *their* growing pleasure as they come to understand that learning can be discovery. Meanwhile, the same list, less the group level, is given to the pupils, who are asked to cooperate with each other. If Sammy is writing about George Washington and comes across material on George Washington University (Steve's topic), he can direct Steve to those sources. This is the kind of sharing we want to foster in the schools.

An introduction to the library is arranged, and the teacher and her class meet with the librarian, who illustrates the use of the card catalogue, reference room, etc. The mistaken procedure has been to hold such classes in isolation, with the object of orienting students as speedily as possible. At the very beginning of the year, a high school freshman may get to enter the sanctum, meet the high priest or priestess in charge, stare at the forbidding walls of musty knowledge, be shown enough about reference card systems to mystify him (and persuade him to give the library as wide a berth as possible thereafter); and that's that. Maybe months elapse before he is called upon to make use of the facilities. Under RPL, there is immediate follow-up: the children enter the library already in the knowledge that a project has been assigned to them. They will go back that day, or the next, or by the end of the week. And the librarian is no longer the grim figure behind a desk, muttering to herself as she catalogues books, either sibillating stern reproofs through her teeth or ungraciously responding to an inquiry. She has become a collaborator. Nothing encourages the student more than to have her say, "Johnny, you're researching frogs, aren't you? Well, I came upon some fascinating articles the other day— I've put them on the reserve shelf for you. Did you know that frogs can pop up in desert potholes just hours after a rainfall—even after years of drought? *I* didn't!"

You might ask whether intelligent preparation and cooperative spirit need only come about under RPL? There is, perhaps, no inherent reason why this should be so. It would be wonderful were all teachers to introduce the library in our manner, properly channel students in its use, and enlist the active and enthusiastic help of the staff; but it simply doesn't often happen without the RPL structure. RPL's distinctive approach is to personalize education for every child, with the effect of also fostering a personal commitment by the teacher. The student is given initiative. From his free choice of what level he will pursue, to the comments he is encouraged to make on his own performance, he is encouraged to become fully responsible. He is kept informed at all stages of his schooling as to what will be asked of him and how he can best go about it. He is an eager student because he is an achieving student, and his teacher quickly becomes involved in his triumphs and set-backs. Neither teacher nor student nor librarian is The Enemy. The RPL system trains the teacher in observing the steps we've described, which are natural corollaries of the whole educational approach.

Librarians, of course, are won over. They respond to the interest manifested by RPL teachers and students

alike, as who wouldn't? They enjoy a respect that they
have not been accustomed to. They are no longer drag-
ons who hiss and hush for silence—long-nosed gum-
suckers with false teeth whose breath smells of mint
candy—or even warehouse workers, indistinguishable
from the dust on the shelves. They become allies of
RPL students and teachers, co-authors of the projects,
which they themselves have had a hand in formulating. They seek out references that enrich a student's
research. In consultation with the project teacher, they
purchase additional source books. A librarian's budget
is always limited. Knowing beforehand what students
will be coming to her for is a wonderful help when she
orders. Librarians working with Ramseur System
classes take the initiative of notifying the teacher
when new materials of personal or class interest have
come in, and they are more than happy to co-operate in
planning library periods for students, which eases
their own schedules. They know that they can, in
turn, expect of RPL-trained teachers (1) advance
information on what may be needed, (2) tips on what's
currently available, (3) thorough indoctrination of
students in the use of library books or articles for class
work, (4) assistance with reading guidance, and,
finally, (5) information regarding the interests, needs,
and abilities of the children who will be coming to
them.

There's crabgrass in every lawn, and in every dozen
or so eggs there's likely to be a bloodspot, but the
experience of librarians with RPL has generally been
a happy one.

> It has been a pleasure [wrote one] working with RPL
> students. . . . They are happy students with a goal that
> they can realize. The teachers have become more aware of

the library and know they must utilize . . . its facilities if they are to be successful RPL teachers. By working with the teachers in planning projects and research for students, I am always aware of what is going on in the classroom. In the past, I have seen students grow to hate the library because they were given work they were not capable of doing. Now they find [it] helpful and enjoyable. My circulation of materials doubled after the RPL system became a part of the school system.[2]

RPL teachers and librarians together can endow a school library with the climate of a true learning center—one that excites instead of adding to the tedium of unimaginative teaching, and one that inspires respect instead of abuse and disdain. This mutual effort to focus on quality of work helps everyone concerned in choosing research materials more wisely and thereby permits a wider range and variety. As budgets get smaller, as they become correspondingly tighter, the sensible RPL approach to library work becomes more pertinent.

Footnotes, Chapter VII

[1] Mary Virginia Clark, in a written evaluation of RPL, 1969.

[2] Mary Virginia Clark, in a written evaluation of RPL in January, 1971. Mrs. Clark helped us to design the library role in Ramseur System. She was the librarian of Camden High School from 1964–69.

Chapter VIII
Guidance: A Helping Hand

Three elements of student guidance • Estrangement between teachers and counselors • RPL's answer to more effective counseling

Generally speaking, teachers have a low opinion of student counselors. We won't surmise about the opinion counselors may have of teachers.

But what bases do these people have for the wisdom they supposedly dispense? How do they arrive at the psychological insights that inform them about the best direction a child should take? Grades and rank, as we have already shown, are often meaningless. Course titles do not reveal differences in teachers' requirements and their manner of marking. Written evaluations frequently parrot stereotyped or overly simplified explanations of student performance. The task is too critical to be handled by any one individual or without standardized and objective criteria.

For student guidance to do any good, three elements must be harnessed to pull at the same time: trained personnel, teachers, and the students themselves. The traditional function of counselors has been to administer various testing programs, point students toward appropriate colleges and universities, identify pupils who need psychological help or special programs of instruction, and themselves treat behavior problems.

Many counselors, however, are required to devote a

large portion of the school day keeping student records and scheduling classes, because the school lacks money, facilities, and staff. This leaves little time for actual counseling. As a result, the gap—that mutually low esteem between counselor and teacher—may grow wider, and each carries out his duties as though there were no common purpose.

The counselor is, in theory, a haven for the troubled student. In guidance training programs, theorists caution against acting as a disciplinarian too, the rationale being that it is difficult, if not impossible, for a counselor to play the father confessor for a student he has just read the riot act to. Although the teacher may comprehend this position, he naturally resents that the counselor does not have to shoulder the same ground and hall duty that is inflicted on faculty, particularly when a teacher's own effectiveness is very much impaired by extraneous obligations consuming his time and energy and tending to dissipate the calm good humor that is so vital to his rapport with students. In schools that draw a distinction between the guidance and teaching staffs, the teacher often begins to view counselors as people who have exchanged the battlefield of the classroom for comfortable private offices where they while away the hours filing papers when they are not admonishing little hooligans to be tolerant of the benighted teacher who has misunderstood them. Unfair as the generalization may be, to many of us, the guidance staff is that happily insulated elite who dream up new forms and reports for which working-stiff teachers will be responsible, shunting off on them part of the counselor's job.

RPL has helped bridge this estrangement by incorporating in its design a guidance program that

simultaneously relieves and facilitates the task of
counselors. As you remember, at the beginning of the
school year and at the end of each reporting period,
every student is closely interviewed. A lot of counseling gets done right here. These student-teacher conference periods are strictly focused on the child in
relation to his work. They are not frivolous probes into
his personal life. The teacher is a willing listener. The
child is his main concern, but that concern is cir-
cumscribed to his educational progress in math, or
French, or whatever subject he is taking. If the student
wishes to discuss problems that have originated outside the class but that he feels have had some bearing
upon his work, he is free to do so. He may *volunteer*
personal matters, but he is not *asked* about them. If he
feels a need to blame his failure on others or on some
external cause, he will be heard out with sympathy
and may be advised to choose another group until he is
able to iron out his difficulties. He is, however, only so
advised on the evidence recorded in his folder material, his grade sheet, and his own comments. He must
make the final decisions.

The instructor may document these sessions for future use, *provided the student does not object.* The
comments of both teacher and student are written on
his grade sheet, in the presence of the student, and
with his permission. Nowadays, it is probably advisa-
ble to have the student sign his approval. Once the
student knows that he need not fear expressing himself freely and that what he says and the advice he
receives are as confidential as he wishes, he is usually
less defensive. The sessions can be as fruitful as they
are important. They often open new approaches to the
teaching and testing of students generally, because

discussion of impasses with one child may reveal, by extrapolation, weaknesses in the whole scholastic program that the instructor has not been aware of. These revelations can be the basis for conferences between teachers, either to share new knowledge or to seek aid from others in helping a child.

When an apparently intractable situation arises, and the student suffers from consistent failure, and only then, the RPL teacher sends the child's folder and grade sheet to the guidance counselors for analysis. The counselor reviews the material, returning it to the teacher with suggestions based upon hard data and not some personal hunch or some laboratory hypothesis about adolescent behavior in general. The note may state that the student should be performing at a higher level, that he has problems unknown to the teacher, or that, based upon review of all of his records and present standing, the guidance office is arranging for special help, which may include psychoanalysis. The counselor himself finds these records a marvelous help in gaining a comprehensive picture of a student who is treading rough water outside the classroom. Important information about the child accumulates in his folder. This is a boon to the counselor: a lot of the groundwork is done for him and he is freed to exercise his specific training. His desk isn't crowded with problems that teachers should be able to find their own answers to. He gets only the refractory cases, and he is given something to go on. And when teacher and counselor work together in this fashion, in concord, neither is infringing on the other's territory. Eventually they view student guidance as a common ground upon which they meet.

There is yet another advantage built into RPL.

Counseling students requires time and space, both of which are at a premium in public schools today. In alleviation of this problem, the RPL teacher dispatches much counseling in the classroom. Of course, privacy is needed when discussing work with a student, but opportunities are created by extemporizing a sound barrier. Other students are assigned a task that requires a given volume of noise, allowing teacher and troubled child to talk without being overheard. RPL teachers are drilled in one important observance. *Counseling sessions are not to be used for disciplinary purposes.* The student is not being hauled on the carpet. He therefore feels free to discuss these private sessions, if he wishes, with fellow students or his parents, and that can be constructive.

In fact, RPL students frequently do confer with their schoolmates, seeking information or encouragement in making academic decisions. Quite often, the advice of the student's peers is more valuable to him than that of his official counselor, teacher, or even parent. And the student, besides, under RPL, is continually informing himself:

1. *He knows what all groups are doing, and he is involved in all class activities.* He does not have to wait for a guidance period to discuss other possibilities. He can guide himself within the framework of the class.

2. *He may discuss his work and compare assignments with other students* in formulating his decision.

3. *He has access at all times to all levels of materials,* which he can use as "practice" for a stab at a higher group.

4. Since RPL emphasizes a mutuality of interest between students and the school staff, *he is less loath to seek,* or self-conscious about seeking, on his own initia-

tive, *additional guidance*. He is, in effect, the decision-maker. In the final analysis, he is his own counselor.

An RPL student, it bears emphasizing, is treated as a mature human being. Since the burden of decisions concerning his school career is placed on him, he knows that his teachers have faith in his ability to choose wisely. Young people tend to live up to this expectation. They flower under it. In child after child—even the most uncertain, or timid, or withdrawn—we have seen this happen. The Ramseur method of classroom counseling has proved incontestably that students, more often than not, do react in a mature manner when they are made the architects of their own decisions in a climate that encourages and honors self-discipline and grants trust and respect for their ability to assume such responsibilities.

Chapter IX
Communication: Please, Somebody Understand Me

Flexibility of RPL • Successful use in sundry subjects • RPL's emphasis on writing in all courses • Cooperation between English department and other disciplines • Instructor's determination of requirements and groups for his course • The need for increased emphasis on writing.

Can RPL be useful in a typing class as well as in economics? Can RPL benefit both the biology instructor who ordinarily lectures and the one who prefers leading his students to knowledge through seminars?

We believe that the teacher of math, or English, or history, or whatever in every grade is best qualified to select the instructional methods that suit his temperament and purposes. Any system of education should be flexible enough to allow for adjustments according to subject. No system should dictate technique; instead, it should enhance the individual teacher's choice of methods. RPL has the happy virtue of plasticity. It can be molded to the distinctive requirements of all fields of study.

For the past decade and a half, RPL has been successfully employed by specialists in sundry subjects. Our purpose in this book has been to explain the framework of the method so that teachers can apply it to the broadest spectrum of courses. We won't, however, detail the application of RPL in every subject under the sun, which would be needlessly repetitive. Instead, we want to stress the major opportunities offered by our approach in cultivating use of the Queen's English. It is here where public education, to the despair of parents and teachers alike, seems to be failing so egregiously. It is here that the Ramseur method—the other virtues we've claimed for it notwithstanding—proves its greatest worth in the restoration of literacy.

It is not possible for a student under the Ramseur System to graduate as a "functional illiterate." (What, in Heaven's name, is functional about being illiterate?) The whole approach, which is one of quality and achievement in relation to capacity, encouraging the best effort of which students are able and a *modus operandi* of co-operative responsibility among their teachers, ensures against this tragedy.

Th RPL student who cannot keep up at higher levels because he has difficulty expressing himself can demonstrate in Group 3, in courses other than English, what he has learned without having his grade walloped for compositional errors. In his English class, nevertheless, this same student will be taught clear pronoun reference, parallelism, sentence structure variation, and so forth, just as Group 1 and 2 students are, but he will be graded on the more fundamental grammatical norms, such as correct use of *was* and *were* and *he* and *him*. Groups 1 and 2 students are expected to display command of the English language in all its usages, whether literary or technical, and in all courses. We do not claim that they will write with grace and style, but write they will, and correctly. If the student has acquired this ability, he is relieved of

exercise drills—but only then. Since Group 1 and 2
students must ferret out material beyond that discussed in class or included in textbooks, they must also
learn how to research and write up their notes. Written
assignments for these two groups in history or the
natural sciences will underscore that acceptable English is not abandoned outside English class. The
English teacher confers with his colleagues in other
fields about assigning written work for RPL students.
At the same time, RPL teachers of subjects other than
English list the errors most frequently made by their
changes, thereby guiding the English teacher in what
needs to be stressed. A history teacher reports that
definitions of terms invariably begin, "The Council of
Trent was when . . ."; a health teacher complains about
students who introduce a list of causes with, "Three
reasons for obesity are overeating. Another cause
is . . ."; and a physical science instructor asks, "Is there
a new rule that requires at least one capital letter in
every five words?" This cooperation between the English department and other disciplines helps to prevent redundancy in assignments and class work. If a
student has a special interest in science, history, or any
other subject, and wants to excel in Groups 1 and 2, he
is motivated to improve his English; for success at
these two levels depends to a great degree on his
understanding of the language and his ability to express himself in it. Students, moreover, learn from
different courses distinct styles of writing and are
thereby exposed to exercises in creative and formal
expression. An analysis of personality for psychology
class is unlike an analysis of the portrayal of character
in fiction.

The number of groups offered in a course and the

requirements for each may differ to some extent between one discipline and another. Not all subjects contain three groups. A college preparatory class in English composition, for instance, would not include Group 3 because in an advanced writing course there should be no limitations on the amount or style of writing, nor on the value given to correctness of grammar, spelling, coherence, etc. Biology II, modern language at third and fourth year level, advanced mathematics, chemistry, physics and other accelerated courses also would not be offered in Group 3. No student is *denied* the right to register for these courses, but he is told that to receive credit he must do well in Group 2 first. Only if he has been successful in Group 2 or 1 in previous courses will he be advised to enroll in the advanced ones.

We tend to forget that even in mathematics clear English is essential. Euclid's *Elements of Geometry* is the oldest textbook in the world, having influenced man's ideas for over two thousand years. This goes for other disciplines. Le Corbusier is as regarded for the elegance of his style as for the elegance of his buildings, and Churchill and De Gaulle may be more generously remembered for their histories and memoirs than for their careers as statesmen.

We don't, of course, intend to wax literary about a plumber's wrench. Vocational courses may make use of the RPL division into groups but do not require nearly as much written expression. In addition to more stringent speed and accuracy standards for Group 1 and 2 typing students, for example, a child in Group 2 should also be required to convey in writing his knowledge of the parts of the typewriter or the correct forms of address, while a child in Group 1 will himself compose some of the letters to be typed by the class. There are vocational students in machine shop who seem to have a special talent for designing tools or drafting plans, and there are others whose talents lie in the use of the tools and an understanding of how to follow the blueprints. Each learns according to his bent.

The instructor determines the number of groups in his class and the requirements for each. The biology teacher decides to include Group 3 because he believes that even a student who is unable to write good English can benefit from learning about his body and the world around him. The typing teacher determines the number of words per minute a Group 2 student should master. But RPL imposes an overall structure. RPL insists that the teacher's requirements be clearly defined and that there be some writing for all Group 1 and 2 students, because a certain amount of uniformity is necessary to assure equal work and reward for everyone, and there is also the need to keep an eye on the effectiveness of teachers. Each year, through practice and study, RPL teachers alter, add, or delete certain requirements to improve the standards of every level of instruction.

The emphasis we place on writing—our insistence on it—derives from our distress over the progressive deterioration in the use of language during this past decade. Man, after all, thinks in words, speaks words, and writes words. A limited vocabulary handicaps not only communication but thought itself, and the bad thing about solecisms in any language is that they obstruct the clear and accurate transmission of what the mind conceives and wishes to express. (In an emergency, this can be critical. "General, the second battalion that's in the orchard grove, is pinned down."

"Captain, we have five battalions in your sector. Do you mean the 2nd Battalion, which is in the orchard grove, or do we have two battalions in that grove and is it only the second of them that's pinned down? If I order an air strike, will we be unloading on our own men?") While politicians keep flattering young people (future voters) by assuring them they are the smartest generation ever, statistics on literacy reveal that whatever may be their native intelligence, they are severely handicapped in the use of it. Despite the sorry evidence, nevertheless, totems of the educational bureaucracy continue to report remarkable results from the plethora of new (and expensive) programs that boast of teaching Johnny how to read and write.

What we know is this. The programs haven't worked. Johnny remains a tongue-stuck stammerer who gets by with a vocabulary of fewer than two hundred words—some say half that—which he fills out with grunts, grimaces, physical contortions, and you-know-what-I-means. The hard fact is, our schools are turning out millions of literarily crippled graduates every May and June. One of the most revealing pieces we've seen on this scandal was published in *Newsweek* two years ago. Reporting the calamitous nationwide statistics on literacy, and quoting some of America's outstanding scholars on the matter, the article discusses effects on business and industry as well as the plight of graduate schools that have enrolled students who cannot spell, punctuate, or organize their thoughts. There are educators to whom creative writing is such a shibboleth that they discourage nitpicking about grammatical construction because this might stifle spontaneity.[1] *Newsweek* interviewed Dr. Eliott Anderson, professor of English at Northwestern University, who reported that many high school teachers have simply stopped correcting poor grammar and sloppy syntax. It has been established that a course in creative writing is valuable in any secondary school, but Dr. Anderson is ". . . inclined to think that these . . . teachers have subverted their goals. You don't get very interesting creative results," he notes, "from teachers who can't use the language as a tool in the first place."[2] Some teachers have adopted the philosophy that total freedom of expression without regard for the rules of composition is tantamount to creativity; many others, however, stoutly hold that correct usage of the English language is basic to all subjects—for which they are criticized. What monsters such fuddyduddies are! One Harvard freshman who was required under a correctional program to write simple, clear sentences and to arrange them in orderly fashion said, "It nearly drove me crazy. I tried to write what I was really feeling, and I got all these irrelevant comments about grammar all over the pages. I ran through the streets of Cambridge weeping."[3]

There are educators—*educators*—who are inclined to ease the anguish of such poor, persecuted creatures. The Conference on College Composition (which represents 3,000 English professors) voted to "uphold the right of students to their own language." Most educators are not so asinine. John Gabel, head of the English Department at Ohio State University, said that this condoning of anarchy in language ". . . is broad enough to wipe out even the need to learn how to spell. That's misplaced humanism, not education."[4]

Dr. Russell Kirk, for nearly three decades in the forefront of the battle against the collapse of standards, wondered publicly whether it wouldn't be nice if young people could spell their own names. He wrote about a freshman at the University of Montana who plainly could not. "Atop the one quiz he managed to take in my 'Introduction to the Study of Religion,' he wrote 'Mike Anerson,' with a heavy smudge around the error. He had evidently tried more than one spelling and settled on this one. A fluke? Consider his answer to the principal test question—James Baldwin's *Go Tell It on the Mountain*. It read: 'Pick a character from the novel and tell why, in your opinion, he/she was/wasn't saved.' The answer read: 'Roy and John of Deb the first wife of Gabriel, were drinking wines and smokeing and doing many things' (sic)."[5]

That was in 1975. Two years later, Professor Kirk despairingly reported, "Despite all the talk . . . of 'crash programs' to enable young people to read and write, and despite very large sums expended by federal and state governments to achieve that worthy end, all the indices show that functional literacy continues to decline."[6]

One, probably the major, cause for laxness in demanding correct use of language is the philosophy that all children are capable of learning anything that is properly taught, and if they don't, it is the teacher's failure to teach properly. It follows that failing grades are frowned on by administrators; the teacher must account for them. One way of decreasing the number of strike-outs is to avoid going to bat on anything difficult, such as writing. The teacher has resorted to the multiple-choice test, which is the equivalent of giving drivers a multiple choice at a traffic light.

Another cause for the decreased emphasis on writing is the importance placed on "behavioral objectives." These have become a must in education. A behavioral objective has to be measurable. For instance, to be able to repair a radio qualifies because it can be demonstrated by actually repairing a radio. To know how an amplifier works does not qualify because a person cannot prove that he knows. He may draw one, or put one together, but that does not prove that he knows how it works.[7] (For his gravitational field theory, which he could not "demonstrate," Albert Einstein would have been given a zero.) We have extracted the example of the radio from Robert F. Mager's *Preparing Instructional Objectives,* a text that explains how student achievement is gauged under the behavioral approach and the great virtues thereof. We respectfully demur. To confine a person to listing facts, turning a knob, or repairing transistors in order to measure his achievement makes a mechanic of everyone. Language, of course, deteriorates. One picture may be worth a thousand words, but we happen to believe that a good poem is worth a thousand books on such preposterous nonsense as this. Truth and insight are properties of the imagination, discovered in the word and by the word alone transmitted from the mind of the thinker to humanity at large. The utterly mechanistic approach of behavioral objectives not only reduces culture to the application of the previously discovered—the application of principles—but militates against new discoveries. Civilization wasn't built on the pocket calculator that blissfully relieves us of the drudgery of long division. It was built on an understanding of long division and microelectronics. It was built on the Arab discovery of the principle of zero around twelve hundred years ago, which is a theoretical value proceeding from a logical ordering of the conceptual processes. Language is not only the prime expression of those processes; language—thought symbols—germinates those processes. Noam Chomsky's remarkable insight that a sense of grammar ("generative grammar," he calls it) is built into all human beings, even the deaf and dumb in the structure of their sign language,[8] is another way of saying that grammar is an integral quotient of humanity. Rob children of developing this innate sense, and you are robbing them of a constituent that defines them as human.

In an English course the student must learn the parts of speech to understand how words are put together in order to convey meaning. To use words as tools of communication, he must learn to spell them, pronounce them, and deploy them. He will only acquire these skills through exercising them, and he will exercise them more frequently when their use is demanded. He can memorize the elements of language but not an understanding of them, which is the crucial point. Yet understanding is not a "behavioral objective" because it is not measurable.

Many teachers are required to present behavioral objectives to their administrators at the beginning of each school term. These may or may not be read by the principals. The assumption is that the objectives were satisfied if there are few or no failures in the course. Rarely is a teacher asked to explain the absence of failures. Parents, naturally, don't ask why the grade is good or how it was earned. They should. Behavioral objectivists contend that questions under this method can elicit broad answers that require a knowledge of writing. We just don't buy it. In fact, we challenge anyone to purchase Mager's book, study it, and design questions after his prescriptions that do not relegate the student to the lowest cognitive level.

Philologist Mario Pei, along with other language experts, defines another major villain as the school of "structural linguistics," which asserts that writing is far less important than speech. Pei maintains that "teachers in the classroom have come increasingly under the sway of the structured linguistic dogma; that the spoken idiom is superior to the written, and that there is no real need for students to study the rules of their language."[9] Again, teachers are blamed for an approach that in most cases has been imposed on them to the detriment of education in this country. Mr. Pei, and all others who are worried about the state of American public schooling, must recognize one very important thing: teahers are usually told what to do, not asked. They follow the directives of their superior, who received them from his superior, who acquired them from professors of education, who in turn adopted them from theorists in castellated towers up above that ring of fleecy pink clouds that obscures the real educational world from Parnassus. A great number of teachers are disheartened, dismayed, disgusted, and despairing over the collapse of our public schools. They do not like to see standards undermined, but they feel they are helpless to prevent the sappers from their work.

Yet another blow to English—"that amber in which a thousand precious and subtle thoughts have been safely embedded and preserved,"[10]—has come from supporters of "Students' Right to Their Own Language," of which the Conference on College Composition and Communication is one lobby. We are second to none in the delight we take when we run across some particularly vivid expression in the vernacular of children, particularly the black children with whom we are so familiar. There can be dazzling imagistic effects. There can be a wonderful originality and forcefulness. We are indebted to W. M Woods, of Oak Ridge, Tennessee, for the following example. He writes:

> It was in Louisville, Kentucky, I believe, back in 1938 or 1939, that I heard and collected my most multiply negative expression. I was a very young chemical engineer, trying to help Seagram make whisky fit for human consumption. I rented a room from Colonel Thompson, who owned two large old antebellum-style houses, next to each other, the rooms of which he rented to bachelors like me. Colonel Thompson was a typical Kentucky colonel: white mustaches, string tie, immaculate shirt, threadbare but well-pressed suit, a liking for mint juleps, and an entirely undependable memory. When hard-pressed for liquid funds, one could put off paying the Colonel the room rent for several months by suggesting that he had been paid, but had simply forgotten.
>
> The Colonel employed a little black boy . . . perhaps thirteen or so years old to do odd jobs. Among other tasks assigned to him, this boy was supposed to keep the Colonel's shoes shined. To be able to shine shoes one must have shoe polish, and the boy had reminded the Colonel several times that he was about out of shoe polish, that he needed a new supply if the shoe shining operation was to continue. In his usual forgetful fashion, the Colonel promptly disremembered, and failed repeatedly to replenish the boy's supply of polish.
>
> In this context, I came upon the boy sitting on the back stoop trying to polish the Colonel's shoes. He was digging

the last remnants of polish out of the corners of the tin, trying to eke out, and muttering aloud to himself. He did not see me, so I eavesdropped.

This is what he said, verbatim: "Won't nobody never buy nobody nothing to do nothing with, can't nobody never do nothing for nobody, nohow."

The syntax may have been flawed, but the semantical content was quite plain. I went out and bought him half a dozen tins of polish with my own money.

Southern-born that we are, we also know exactly what the boy meant (better—the genius of his use of language—exactly how he was *feeling* at the time); but in a world that is growing smaller, with people forced to exist in close contact, greater than ever is there a need for intercommunication. Nevertheless, there still exist educators in high position who promote the acceptance of any and all dialects, accusing those of us who insist on basic standard language of discrimination against ethnic minorities. The teacher is expected, and sometime directed, to tolerate any illiterate usage by which the student is accustomed to expressing himself, and never mind the consequences. The argument that some people have not been exposed to good English in their homes and neighborhoods, and that it is therefore "unfair" or "discriminatory" to repair that handicap, contradicts the major purpose of education, which is to elevate a nation's culture. What other justification is there?

The rationales behind all these faddish theories belie common sense. Meanwhile, young people suffer. One wonders why anyone would frivolously deny our children the single tool that links them to the past and without which the chances for a productive future are seriously compromised.

Footnotes, Chapter IX

[1] "Why Johnny Can't Write," *Newsweek,* December 8, 1975, p. 60.

[2] *Ibid.,* p. 60.

[3] "Too Many A's," *Time,* November 11, 1974, p. 106.

[4] *Ibid.,* p. 106.

[5] John A. Miles, Jr., "Variations on a Theme," *National Review,* July 18, 1975.

[6] Russell Kirk, "Illiterate Collegians, *"National Review,"* February 3, 1978, p. 158.

[7] Robert F. Mager, *Preparing Instructional Objectives,* Fearon Publishers, Palo Alto, California, 1962, pp. 19–20.

[8] N. Chomsky, *Syntactic Structures,* New York: Humanities Press, Inc., 1957; Chomsky, N., *The Biological Fondations of Language,* Lennenberg, E. H. (ed.), Cambridge, Mass.: The M.I.T. Press, 1967.

[9] "Why Johnny Can't Write," *op. cit.*

[10] Richard C. Trench, Nineteenth Century Archbishop, philologist, theologian and poet. England.

Chapter **X**
Teachers: Respected and Rejected

Teacher complaints • Measure of teacher efficiency
• Weaknesses in methods of evaluating teacher effec-
tiveness • Ramseur method of assaying teachers'
worth • The protection of the teacher and the school
under the RPL method of appraisal • Teacher
abuse • Restoration of professionalism

Parent: "Raise teachers' salaries? Why, most of them are making more now than they deserve. What can I say to my son Jim about his careless mistakes in history when his teacher writes on the report card, 'Jim has *stop studing* this reporting period.' "

Parent: "I don't understand why my daughter Alice is making a "C" in a tenth grade accelerated English class when one of her friends who has always just skimmed by is making a "B" in the remedial English class."

Teacher: "What's Mr. Jamison's secret? How does he rate having only college preparatory courses? Who can't be successful, teaching the bright students? Being complimented every year on what a remarkable job I have done doesn't change the fact that the records show a wide discrepancy in progress between his students and mine. How can we be held equally accountable for success that naturally comes more easily for him?"

Teacher: "Mr. Owen may be the principal, but how can he possibly judge my knowledge of French when his only training has been as a physical education teacher. Besides, when he visited the classroom, the hour was devoted to reports by the *students* on French culture, not by me."

Student: "Mrs. Allan can't be much of a teacher. She gets only the slow students."

These are stock complaints from within and without public schools. Some may be sound, others not. There are whiners in any profession. There are poor teachers who should be rooted out, and we would guess that the quality of teachers becomes progressively more doubtful below the age of fifty, commonsurate with the progressive decline of the educational standards that they studied under. But there are also thousands upon thousands of diligent and devoted teachers in this country who travail in the most trying conditions, who would like to see public education regain its self-respect, who do not get the credit they deserve, and whose frustrations year by year mount. We're not a bit hesitant, immodest as it may be, to count ourselves in the second group, and we believe that the Ramseur System can eliminate at least some of the injustices that teachers have solid reason to complain about. To begin with, RPL goes a long way in separating the sheep from the goats.

No system of education in itself will ever rid the schools completely of substandard teachers or always reward the deserving. RPL, however, as well as manifesting strengths, exposes professional weaknesses that the school authorities and, in the last analysis, parents also can act upon. RPL minimizes incongruities that engender bitterness and disillusionment.

Nothing is more infuriating to the conscientious and capable teacher than to be classed as a "subprofessional[1] . . . who is not fighting battles for the sake of children but is thinking of himself,"[2] and to be trapped in a situation that does not recognize dedication and ability, placing him at the mercy of subjective and, more often than not, unfair judgments of his competence.

How can efficiency in the transmission of knowledge—which is as much art as skill—be measured? Who taught better, Socrates or Aristotle? Yet if schools are to provide an education, they must be able to weigh the pedagogical ability of their faculty. Although every staff position is vital, it is the teacher who is the linchpin; paradoxically, of all those on a school's payroll, he is the most difficult to rate. If the building is clean and equipment functions, the custodian has earned his wages. If the records are up-to-date and all letters have been typed and signed, the secretarial staff is doing its job. The principal, supervisors, and superintendent are given high or low marks by the community at large, though this is often a political matter, because the public generally comes to an opinion about these officeholders based on their own estimations of their work. The teacher, on the other hand, has no means of blowing her trumpet. The yardsticks that measure devotion are difficult to come by. Those that measure competence are shot through with defects.

This places principals in a jam. How are they to improve the quality of their faculty? Performance of some duties can be fairly easily assessed. Being on the job at the right time and promptly completing assigned book work is either a teacher's practice or not. But alleging incompetence or an uncooperative attitude to a teacher by reliance on current methods of evaluation is next to impossible. It becomes a political matter. The profession has its lobbies too. The National Teacher's Association has become the bulwark of the mediocre, and the charge of racism is leveled whenever the criticized instructor happens to be black or Mexican or belongs to some other locally sensitive minority. Unless the principal is able to prove insubordination, it is extremely difficult to refuse renewing a contract. RPL, as you'll see, takes him off this book.

Miss Jonas, not versed in her field, presented a particularly sad spectacle when she was assigned an accelerated ninth grade English class. She pronounced the plural of stewardess to be *stewardi* and explained that the noun, *feelings* (as of someone's), had to be concrete, since it (or they?) referred to one of the senses. Students amused the community with her eccentricities. She was, in fact, as qualified to teach English composition as Hagar the Horrible to lead the Northern Renaissance. She became the talk of the town. This ridicule rubbed off on the rest of the faculty. Some parents felt that if Miss Jonas had to teach—if there were no way of easing her out—less harm would be done to bright students because they were aware of her curiousness and were already ahead of her in the subject. But what about the year they lost that, under a competent teacher, could have taken them further? Though students suffer from these cases, the image of all professionals is tarnished. The skilled teacher's morale is demolished because there is no distinction drawn between her and the Miss Jonases.

Why can't our schools correctly scale those teachers who are doing their jobs well and those who either cannot or won't? Why do well-meaning principals who sincerely want to put together the best possible faculty throw up their hands? It's the unsatisfactory set of yardsticks used in assessing competence that stymies them. It is their unreliability and, very often, their unfairness—which is universally recognized—that is ruinously eroding faculty morale. Good teachers do not get justice; indifferent teachers do not get their desserts.

The most common way of rating a teacher is through classroom observation. Someone in authority audits a class for one hour a month; or an hour a semester; or, more likely, an hour a year. For all the benefit derived, this is an utter waste of time. Principal, assistant principals, heads of departments, and people from other schools or the state department of education are usually tapped for the task. Each has his particular field of interest and is not necessarily qualified in other disciplines. In some cases, a former instructor of drivers' education may be the one to judge an English or chemistry teacher's appearance, presence, effectiveness, and knowledge. ("Miss Adams applied too much clutch with some students while not braking hard enough with others. She seems to have no talent for parallel parking."[3]) Often, like most people, the evaluator has preconceived ideas about what constitutes good teaching, and even instructors in the same field of study will differ on method. In the transmission of knowledge, every good teacher, according to his temperment, has a special and very personal way of presenting the material to students. Some are fine lecturers; others use audio-visual aids with brilliant effect. As in the case of inductive vs. deductive methods, who is to say which is best? Certainly it would be a dull school that admitted of no variation.

Were one observer to do all the rating, at least consistency could be achieved, but when more than one person is responsible for appraising the faculty, methodological preferences and arbitrary standards invalidate the results. Mr. Dunn, the principal of a neighboring high school, gave no superior ratings to the teachers he reviewed; but Mr. Cass, the assistant principal, was prodigal with them. It was Mrs. Quinn's lot to be selected by Mr. Dunn for observation. The report he wrote on her was predictably middling. To Mrs. Quinn, this was inequitable, because she knew that right down the hall Mr. Cass was handing out superiors with his amiable regularity. But when she remonstrated with her principal, pointing out the unfairness, he replied that he did not believe in superior ratings because he did not believe anyone was perfect. "That's just dandy," she said, "but your assistant principal *does* believe that some of us can be star teachers, and I'm being compared with colleagues in my own subject who are lucky enough to draw him for an observer. Besides, why *have* a superior in the form at all if you don't believe anyone can possibly qualify for such a rating?" Her protest was unavailing. The capricious report on her effectiveness entered Mrs. Quinn's file, an unjust but permanent record.[4]

The glaring defects of observation have led educators to seek more deterministic methods. Flander's Factor Analysis was designed to judge the "classroom climate" that promotes an environment conducive to teaching and learning. Other educators, Donald M. Medley, Edward J. Amodon, and Arthur Combs among many, have set up check lists of desirable characteristics to be looked for in teachers. Johnny answers a question. The teacher smiles at him. (Desirable—one check mark.) She gently pats him on the head. (Desirable—one check mark.) If she is familiar with the analysis system, she will be smart to pat and smile simultaneously. (Two check marks!)

There are two major weaknesses here: the observer is still going to view the behavior of the teacher on the basis of his preconceived ideas, and students do not react in a normal manner when there is a stranger in their midst. (Anyone who is not a permanent member of the class can be classified as a stranger.) John Holt author of the popular book *How Children Fail,* observed,

> "Their [students'] attention depended on what was going on in the class. Classroom observers don't seem to see much of this. Why not? Some of them do not stay with a class long enough for the children to begin to act normally in their presence. But even those who are with the class for a long time make the mistake of watching the teacher too much and the children too little.[5]

But let's suppose the analysis system works. Let's suppose that fear of earning a low count on someone's sugar and spice list encourages the approved mannerisms in an entire faculty. Imagine all teachers acting in the same artificial way—smiles, pats, winks, God knows what—like so many identical puppets dancing on the end of strings pulled by Flanders, Medley, Combs, *et al.* As a matter of fact, most of us do smile, pat little heads, wink conspiratorially, chuck chins, swab runny noses, extract splinters, tell suitable innocuous jokes, praise, pet, and even sometimes scold. We do this naturally and spontaneously and according to our instincts as teachers and as adults who happen to be very fond of children. If not, we're in the wrong profession.) But such a contrived system of evaluation, were it successful, promotes no more than standardization on the gooiest and most superficial levels. The analysis method promotes sociological convention, not substance—and the property of excellence is the latter.

We agree with the good intentions behind attempting to appraise the merits of teachers. Quality teaching demands quality teachers, but the art of the profession is too elusive to be captured exclusively by one-shot classroom observation or by check lists. More concrete, objective, and substantial criteria are essential. RPL operates under the philosophy that no single method of evaluation can give a true profile of teaching ability. As William W. Purkey states, ". . . we create the people we see. None of us can view the world, or each other, with objectivity, for our perceptions are inexorably filtered through our experience."[6] A fair critique requires that all who are a part of the educational program be involved. The teacher must be a participant in the process and not merely the subject of review.

The Ramseur method of assaying a teacher's worth, as in the case of students, is mainly by self-evaluation. This may sound fishy, but hold on, here is how it works and how it leads to an objectivity accurate record of a teacher's abilities.

The RPL teacher measures himself against the goals he has set for his students. Is he reaching students of different capacities? Is he testing the skills that the students of each group must acquire? Does his grading reveal their achievement and, at the same time, by annotation, does it serve as a further aid to teaching and learning? To all such questions there must be positive answers, because failure in any one of these areas will cause failure in the others. If an instructor is unsuccessful in teaching to all levels, this will be revealed in his testing and grading, and, conversely, if his testing and grading are not designed to reach each group, his methods will be negatively reported by his supervisor. Therefore, teacher and pupil are both profiled by the same material—the student's folder, grade sheet, and permanent record. Since this file is open to review by the student, his parents, administrators, any supervisor, and colleagues on the faculty, the teacher is in fact, at the conclusion, evaluated by all, but he will be the first to determine whether he has the necessary knowledge and ability. He cannot hide his failings from anyone, least of all himself.

A teacher has become an RPL teacher by choice. The optimum situation of course, as we've said, would be a school where every member of the faculty taught under the Ramseur concept and all students and instructors were rated the RPL way. But when this doesn't hold, RPL will, in the meantime, allow the dedicated and knowledgeable professional to function in any school without conflicting with other systems. RPL can only help. It cannot harm.

We are sympathetic with teachers who back away from one other *method.* We have been bombarded by, and involuntarily enlisted in, so many wondrous new answers to educational woes that we are ourselves method shy. But, believe us, no teacher of ability need fear RPL, only the lazy or incompetent. When a teacher takes on the demanding standards we've set forth, he has agreed to follow the system's procedures and to stand or fall on that basis. This is not only implicit in his commitment; it is inherent in the requirements of RPL. The teacher does not lose his freedom. His personality has full rein; he can still prefer Socrates to Aristotle, seminars to lectures. He, alone, decides what materials he will use and what demands (special to his subject) he will place on his students and himself. He contracts, however, that he will teach to *all* his students, *regardless* of native capacity; that he will test and grade students' work on the level they have chosen; and that he will make student data available to those who have the right to be concerned with his performance, whether his superior or a worried parent. This does not dispense the teacher from classroom observation, which in cases can be a useful auxilliary; but he will be protected from any subjective inadequacies of such appraisal. If he is doing a good job, the RPL grading system and student records will show it, despite what some ex-coach may think.

By no means do we claim for the Ramseur System that it can make a weak teacher strong, an uncooperative teacher cooperative, an apathetic teacher enthusiastic, and an undedicated teacher dedicated. What RPL does, however, is to reveal to all pertinent parties, most importantly the person under review himself, what kind of teacher he really is. In recent years, when competency tests have been proposed for students or when the National Teachers' Examination has been enforced for instructors, the matter degenerates immediately into controversy over whether cryptic racism isn't at the heart of the measure. There can be no such charge laid against RPL, which treats students and teachers with regard to nothing except their performance (in the case of students, on their performance *at their chosen level*). The black student from an illiterate household can do well and honorably in Group 3, and if he demonstrates native capacity will

promote himself to Groups 2 or 1. He will find white
children in all three groups. The good black teacher
cannot be fired by a redneck board that merely alleges
that he doesn't pass professional muster. He can point
to the record; and if he has been fired for reasons
unsupported by it, he can raise a legitimate howl.
Education, nevertheless, cannot be allowed to become
a haven of last resort for the unemployable or a
battlefield on the front of affirmative action. The person who hasn't the ability to teach all three groups
should be dismissed, whether he is white or black, in
the interest of all children, black or white.

At the risk of repeating, let's. *A capable teacher
whose performance is fairly judged has no reason to
fear being held accountable.* To the contrary, he wel-
comes public insistence on first-rate teaching. Such an
emphasis, along with the hiring and retaining of personnel on the basis of strict merit, provides status that
the teacher today sorely lacks. With everyone free to
pursue whatever profession he wishes, only those who
are capable of doing the job ought to be heading the
classrooms of our schools.

RPL also soothes teachers by eliminating partiality
in the assignment of low level courses, by which they
become identified in the public mind. (Mrs. Allen always gets the dummies; *ipso facto,* Mrs. Allen herself
must be one.) Under RPL, there's no such thing as a
high or low level course.

We confess: we haven't discovered El Dorado for
pedagogs. A career in public education can be like a
career in the Army, where the Spanish-speaking
officer is sent to France or Portugal, but never to Spain
or South America, unless it's Brazil, or where the whiz
at handling men in the field is marooned in a stall

position. Administrative foul-ups are abundant in every profession. Schools, like the Army, never seem to have enough people or the right people, and teachers are subject to what can be, or seem to be, the most obtuse assignments by superiors. RPL is no guarantee against being required to teach a course remotely related to one's field, where one may have to struggle to keep a page ahead of the students; nor against being handed a totally new subject of instruction just a few days prior to the opening of school, allowing no time for preparation. RPL does not promise the teacher that he will be allowed to assess the worthiness of his superiors or the soundness of programs initiated by them.

We've harped on this matter before. It's a sore point. Those who are primarily responsible for the education of the young; those who fill the trenches; those without whom there could be no education and whose experience is immediate, direct, and in most cases invaluable, are ignored when decisions are being made. John R. Morphet, author of *Educational Administration,* has stated what would seem to be obvious:

> The achievement of the school's purposes is dependent upon the extent to which all personnel develop and re-examine certain common goals and genuine satisfaction of participating in working toward them. Any act that causes individuals or groups not to be "in" reduces the likelihood of high attainment of goals.[7]

Teachers are generally "out." They get orders. They are not treated as though they played a part in a mutual endeavor . . . not to mention that theirs is by far the most important part. In case after case, the instructor is invited to contribute little to prescribed policies, the subject matter to be taught, how it will be taught, or the rules that regulate the school from day to day. Why this should be so is beyond comprehension, but the utter disregard is a paramount reason for the disaffection of teachers everywhere.

Maybe even more insulting than being left out of decisions on the curriculum is being disingenuously asked for an opinion that is then totally ignored. In May of 1975, Miss Green and Mr. Usher, high school teachers, along with administrators and faculty from the other county schools, were appointed to serve on a committee whose purpose was to review the overall problems of that area, decoct plans to eliminate them, and create a rapport that would encourage common educational goals. One topic was the reporting of student absences at secondary level. What to do about this was debated at length; what *not* to continue was decided. Policy had been for teachers to telephone parents whose children were chronic truants, bringing the matter to their attention in the vain hope of eliciting their cooperation. But because of the high average number of students each instructor taught, the Curriculum Committee, as it was dubbed, agreed that there was neither time nor were there the facilities to continue the effort. Past experience had proved a miserable failure. Some teachers had been subjected to abusive language. They were called meddlesome and told to mind their own business. Their calls, generally, were about as welcome as the parson's visit to a parishioner at cocktail hour. Even those inquiries that received a polite reception did not improve the attendance record.

You may be of the opinion that the Curriculum Committee made a poor decision when it voted to discontinue telephoning about student absences. Be that as it may, it was arrived at by a majority of fulltime professional teachers who had had long and unsuccessful experience with the old policy. The Curriculum Committee subsequently wrote a statement on this and other recommendations, which was duly presented to the secondary school staffs for approval. There the work rested, and Miss Green and Mr. Usher went back home weary but satisfied that at long last the teaching staff was being included in the formation of policy. But three months later, at the very beginning of the fall term, the principal of City High School blandly informed his faculty that among their duties would be . . . ringing up parents of children who missed more than five days in a reporting period. Stunned, Miss Green and Mr. Usher rose up to ask, "What about the recommendation of the Curriculum Committee?" He replied that he was not aware of any such recommendation and that his directive would be carried out.

We could relate dozens of similar stories, in which the opinions of teachers are first solicited and then given the heave-ho. This is token recognition, and we teachers resent it. Strange as it may seem, we're not, on the whole, stupid, and we classify such treatment for what it is—condescending and placating: formally including us while paying no attention to us, listening to us while not heeding us.

RPL is also helpless to redress another major grievance. Teachers are overloaded. We must be released from duties that are not instructional, that frazzle the unruffled temper that all of us struggle to maintain, and that should belong strictly to the administrative branch or a nonteaching staff. We understand how this came about. As school problems endlessly proliferate,

tasks that do not relate to teaching are delegated more
and more often to the faculty; but these are seriously
hampering the faculty's effectiveness in discharging
its primary obligation.

Teaching has never been measured by hours spent
in the classroom. We know that; we accept it. Teachers
traditionally sponsor student activities; supervise
programs designed to raise money for them; take part
in student-faculty contests; collect funds for class pictures and insurance; sell tickets at athletic events;
oversee the planning, decorating, and chaperoning of
school proms; and organize the graduation ceremony.
For years, we have willingly given the effort and
time that these extra-curricular chores demand, even
though we aren't paid for them. As much as it wouldn't
occur to the school board to remunerate us for such
extras, it wouldn't occur to us to ask.

But there's a limit. So many extrinsic duties are
being loaded on teachers by the administrative staff
that the relationship smacks of master to slave. Fuel
consumption is a problem; teachers, not janitors, are
charged with the responsibility of making certain all
windows are closed. Students decide to launch new
activities, social or athletic, that require the teacher's
presence; the teacher willy-nilly participates. Teachers nowadays are regularly called upon to give up their
work-study periods in order to fill in for an absent
faculty member, accept additional classes or students
in order to save the school the expense of hiring someone else, design fund-raising events for school projects,
conduct testing programs for the guidance department
or for some school official whose pending doctor's
thesis is in need of data, and on and on and *on*.

This would seem sufficient, but now government

brainstorms are burdening the faculty with endless paper work besides. Although there is a designated director and perhaps an assistant and office staff to tend to these bureaucratic incursions, teachers fill out the forms, teachers administer the tests, and teachers compile the figures. If the director is placed under pressure, he passes that pressure on to the faculty. The faculty does the work and the directors of the programs pick up the check.

Look, this is infuriating, apart from being needless and abusive. Imagine being denigrated to a jack-of-all-trades after having spent years and a considerable investment preparing for a specific profession *(teaching)*—one that requires not only graduate work, but lifelong study on one's own time. But that's not all. Nowadays, in addition to everything else, the teacher has become a police officer. She is commonly assigned for a period before school convenes and during her lunch hours on a given number of days to patrol the halls and school grounds. If the teacher is a six foot, two inch male ex-football guard, that's one thing. But our average teacher is a woman, and, also, no Angie Dickinson.

Miss Brady is maybe 5 feet, 4 inches tall, weighs 110 pounds, has never been trained in self-defense (and never dreamed that a black belt in karate would be a necessary credit in her training to become a teacher), carries no weapon, and is stationed in a second corridor far removed from any adult. The passage is 300 feet long. There are three exits that lead to the first floor. There are 12 classrooms, a library, two restrooms, and a teachers' work room. The dimly lit hall has a large window at both ends so that a glance in either direction will show only a silhouette. Her duty is to be there to deter vandalism, prevent theft, protect students from physical harm or extortion, and to keep the passageways clear and allow no students into the lockers along the walls during this period. Restrooms and classrooms are open for the students to use. She must race from one end of the corridor to the other; and as she reaches that end, students will pour into the other behind her or up the middle stairs to their lockers and be on their way before she is able to race back. She feels like the idiot students come to take her for; she begins to feel like Ms. Grundy out of the comic strip, "Archie." She is not physically capable of dedending herself or students in cases of violence. She has no means of contacting anyone for help, and if she did, there are too many avenues by which the culprits can escape long before help arrives.

Such duty degrades her. It is degrading to the whole profession. In the student's eye, teachers become ridiculous, objects of scorn. Miss Brady is not going to keep rude and violent children from victimizing others by her ineffectual presence. To the contrary, her presence encourages such behavior. Certain children delight in practicing vicious traits under the noses of people in authority when those people have become absurd and when they know they can do so with impunity. This lack of respect carries from the no-man's land of the corridors into the classroom. Miss Brady is solving no problems for the school by policing the premises, but in the meantime she has been obliged to assume a function that is undermining her in the job for which she has been trained and hired. It's senseless. Every magazine and newspaper article on violence in the schools ends by stating that officials are cracking down but that nothing seems to work. To use teachers for "cracking down" is about as effective as trying to crack a walnut with a feather.

As we've confessed, RPL is no panacea for the teacher's plight in these and other areas of distress, but RPL does restore professionalism. Good teachers can be confident that the record will prove their worth. Poor teachers are weeded out.

Footnotes, Chapter X

[1] Fenwick English, "The Ailing Principal," *Phi Delta Kappan* (November, 1968), p. 6.

[2] Charles H. Harrison, "AASA Critical of Teacher, Softer on U. S. Involvement," *Education News,* (March 4, 1968), p. 25.

[3] *Nous en excuse.*

[4] Curiously, Mr. Dunn, as a teacher, had been known for lenient grades.

[5] John Holt, *How Children Fail* (New York: Pittman Publishing Corporation, 1964), pp. 20–22.

[6] Wm. W. Purkey, "Perception, Self-Concept, and Academic Achievement," *South Carolina Schools,* XVI (February, 1965), p. 17.

[7] John Reller Morphet, *Educational Administration* (Englewood Cliffs, New Jersey: Prentice-Hall, Inc., 1959), p. 52.

Chapter XI
Principals: Sometimes Saint, Sometimes Sinner

A principal's working day • RPL as a shield for some of his problems: teacher grievances, apple-of-the-eye parents, government busybodies, incompetent teachers, disciplinary matters • The model principal •Qualifications for the position • The value of RPL in selecting a principal

A normal working day has started for Mr. Hawkins, principal of River Valley High School. The time is seven-thirty a.m. when he makes a hurried tour of the school grounds to check on doors and windows and to see whether teachers are at their stations of patrol duty. At seven forty-five, he returns to his office and glances over his appointments for the day. At eight o'clock, he has a conference with Mrs. Boles. Ralph Boles has a second offense slip from his English teacher, Mrs. Calley, and must bring a parent for a heart-to-heart talk before he can be allowed to return to class. There are three other parent-student conferences that are concluded just in time for a meeting at the superintendent's office at nine-thirty, which will last at least an hour. Mr. Hawkins returns at ten forty-five, fifteen minutes late for a meeting he had scheduled with his assistants to discuss plans for their yearly visit to the classrooms to observe the teachers in action. At eleven-thirty, he checks with the school custodian about a break-down in the heating system.

Yet another government report on the ratio of black and white students who play ping-pong is due in the superintendent's office by three o'clock; he dictates a reminder for those teachers who have not turned in their count and has it circulated among the faculty. Two boys have a fight on a bus, and he rushes off to investigate. Fortunately, no one is hurt, but there goes his lunch time.

While gulping down a cup of black coffee and an indigestible "mystery salad," he contemplates how horribly unpopular he is going to be in a few moments. As soon as the school has settled into its afternoon routine, and lectures, discussions, and tests are begun in the different classes—Buzzzz! The monthly fire drill is on. Youngsters come flying out into the corridors and those tests that took teachers so long to compose are now useless. Thinking of the reaction of his faculty, Mr. Hawkins winces, because he knows that they could not care less that he, personally, will be fined by the fire department if such drills are neglected

Having infuriated his staff, he now faces the ire of parents. Two mothers expect Mr. Hawkins to return their calls. They will speak to no one else. Mrs. Dobbs is terribly upset because Rebecca's name was not included in the newspaper account of the science class field trip. Mrs. Topper (making her biweekly call) wants to know if her Percival is in school. "He's a good boy, you know, and so bright, but he just can't make himself go to school on some days. He feels the teachers don't like him. They should pay more attention to students and less to their after school appointments. . . ." Having failed to pacify Mrs. Dobbs and Mrs. Topper (the Mrs. Dobbses and Toppers of this world are *never* pacified), Mr. Hawkins sprints down the hall to take refuge in the teachers' lounge for a coke and a little light chatter with his faculty—but he sprints not fast enough. Mrs. Tate, a substitute teacher, blocks his way for a ten minute up-to-date report on her daughters, former students at River Valley High, and gently reminds him how Mr. Ziembroski, principal at the time, handled all situations in such a marvelous and tactful way. The comparisons are not subtle. Mr. Hawkins escapes her, finally, heading again for the lounge.

Teachers grow quiet as he enters. He senses their resentment as he approaches their circle. They are mad at him today, they were mad at him yesterday, and they will be madder at him tomorrow. "Good afternoon, Mr. Beacham, how is your typing class going this term?" "None of the machines work. I've waited a month for the repairmen." "Good afternoon, Miss Grundy, how is the enrollment looking in French this year?" "What do you expect? Down! Who cares about foreign languages when the administration can't send out a directive in plain English?" End attempt at fraternization. Soon, however, he is getting an unsolicited earful. Mrs. Child: "Speaking of English, what in the world is the department meeting about? I have a dental appointment this afternoon that took me six months to get!" Mr. Sims: "Speaking of directive, it would certainly be nice to spend a little class time teaching rather than filling out forms. What's this about shuffleboard, anyhow?" Mrs. Smitt: "HEW wants us to reach out more to the community. If my classes are this large next year, I *really* will quit." Ms. Sacks, sniffing: "Maybe I'm off the subject, but will this lounge ever be decorated to look less like a waiting room for the next train to Siberia?" Coach Carley: "Ms.

Sacks, we can hardly be waiting to go—*nous avons arrivée!*"

Mr. Hawkins skulks out, aware he is going to invite downright mutiny later that afternoon when he breaks the news that the state Department of Education has once again changed English requirements for secondary schools, obliging him into a pep talk in which he will exhort everyone to pull together even though it is going to take burning the midnight oil for a week (or five) to effect those changes. As he is making that announcement in the conference room, doing his best to ignore the murderous stares of twenty teachers, he imagines what each will be saying about the monstrous Mr. Hawkins at supper, assuming that they are going to have time for supper. His last hours of the day are spent at his desk, slogging through paper work, attempting to sedate his own rebellious stomach with Tums. He goes home, not to enjoy an evening with his family, but to rush through a meal and back to school in order to supervise extra-curricular activities.

We exaggerate? Hardly. We have asked a number of principals to compile a list of their duties. Naming only those that could not be put off for any reason, they included thirty time-consuming routine functions, nineteen of which demand lengthy written reports. Obviously, little time is left for personal contact with teachers and students, without which an administrator becomes isolated. No time at all is left for the kind of fruitful reflection that distinguishes a leader from a mere caretaker. A principal in these nervous times, when schools have been obliged to assume all sorts of sociological responsibilities that formerly did not enter into their domain, is so absorbed by matters of secondary importance that not a few end up para-

noiac, turning into Captain Queegs. If things seem to
be moving smoothly, something must be horribly
wrong. They are so busy correcting procedural errors
and checking to see that state and federal inquiries
into whether parrot fever affects more black than
white children and if *not, how come* more white than
black children get parakeets to make pets out of in
natural history class, that they have little time for
patting a teacher on the back for a job well done; in
fact, they probably aren't aware of the teacher's accomplishment, so fearful are they of Murphy's law. A
principal has to be a phenomenon to deal with all the
petty vicissitudes of his job and still keep in mind that
his primary mission is to run an educational institution.

The position, frankly, is no enviable one. Although
the salary is more comfortable than a teacher's, it, like
theirs, does not begin to compensate for the tasks and
pressures of the office. The office itself can be more
prestigious than real. Many school problems that a
dedicated principal would like to tackle have been
removed in recent years from his provenance. Again,
like teachers, he has too many superiors. He is an-
swerable to the superintendent, to board members, to
state officials, to HEW, and, now, since the recent emphasis on student rights and resulting court cases,
even to the student body. Urgent matters may not be
treated urgently. They must travel through channel
after channel before they can be resolved, and by that
time they have engendered a dozen more crises of
greater urgency than the first. He is Sisyphus, eternally pushing a boulder uphill, eternally in danger of
having it roll back down on him. In minor degree, it is
not too much to say that the Nixon syndrome besets

many people who are appointed to the office and who do not possess the proper qualification, transforming them into suspicious, exhausted, and despotic cranks.

RPL could shield principals from many dangers and time-devouring exigencies if only they knew about it. Here are three ways that come immediately to mind.

1. *Teachers' grievances.*

If there is one thing teachers most despise, it is any notion that the principal is showing favoritism in awarding desirable classes or subjects to a privileged few. Fire drills irritate; the mere suspicion of favoritism plummets faculty morale and relations between faculty and principal.

RPL takes the principal off this lethal hook. It is a "teachers'" system; no class is more desirable than another, because all instructors alike take on a wide range of intellectual and socio-economic backgrounds in each subject.

2. *Apple-of-the-eye-parents.*

Some parents expect the principal to perceive their child as though in him or her the Creator achieved His finest hour. If their little Alice is placed in what they deem to be a class level below her hyperion endowments, the principal is badgered to death. If he yields to one demand, of course, pushing little Alice up the status scale, he will be buried in an avalanche of other special pleadings.

Students place themselves under RPL; there are no high (or low) status classes.

3. *Government busybodies.*

Government is increasingly the matter with public education. HEW is always on the principal's neck, and his neck sometimes gets stretched on the block. For example, since the ESSA program, which has been tormenting principals and teachers for the last eight years, new procedures every fresh school term are enforced to bring students up to par in reading and math.

This is the way it typically goes. HEW at first agrees to the separation of poor students into special classes for this training. To prevent discrimination in their selection, HEW also agrees that standardized test scores alone will determine assignments. Accordingly, the test is administered, children are placed in their proper classes, and the program begins. Everything is hunkydory. But two months later, the principal is advised that the school must report on the ratio of blacks and whites and males and females in these classes. Based on the information, HEW issues new guidelines. Now students themselves must choose the program, not be placed in it. Defining what is or what is not discrimination has become the main thing, reading and math nothing. Through no fault of his own, the principal has possibly earned a black mark with HEW that could prove mortal to his career.

Under RPL, as we have shown, there can be no accusations of racial discrimination in scheduling or in any grouping and grading. The principal is again off the hook.

Two major problems that increasingly plague principals are ridding the staff of competent teachers and disciplining students. Here, RPL is a godsend for the entire administration. In fact, in these two areas alone, the Ramseur System can be the salvation of public schools, many of which are foundering on the reefs of incompetence and violence.

A principal can have his entire working day dissipated by habitual troublemakers. While he remains holed up with miscreants, inspection of daily school routine is neglected; invitations to classrooms programs can't be honored; important conferences with his faculty are put off. Teachers fill the outer office working up a slow boil as they wait to see him, falling behind in their own work. There's no need for this.

RPL teachers are trained not only to expect but to demand good behavior, and the student who does not conform to the rules is removed from class—sometimes permanently. Such no-nonsense punishment has been criticized by people who break out in hives at the very mention of discipline, especially if the child who was subjected to correction happens to be "disadvantaged." After all, he is a hapless product of his environment. His home and neighborhood are not conducive to good conduct, and it is unjust to penalyze him on that account. Precisely assuming that this may be so—that the child has never been taught basic manners or conduct—we do not budge from our insistence on discipline, because that child's only chance of exposure to civilized norms of behavior will be in school. If schools are to have a civilizing influence on "the whole person," they must uphold standards of civility. The Ramseur System takes this view: we in fact do educate "the whole child," culturally as well as intellectually. We therefore expel anyone from class, without distinction, if he persists in intolerable behavior. (He is not expelled from school. A teacher's authority does not extend beyond the classroom.) RPL provides, moreover, a structural atmosphere that encourages good manners. If students have no legitimate grounds for resentment—no legitimate cause for criticizing their placement, no valid complaint about their chances of succeeding in the course, and records to protect them against teacher bias—chips fall from many shoulders. They can get ahead under RPL in their chosen level if they want to, and they know it. They therefore tend to become engrossed in the process of learning, meanwhile picking up the behavioral patterns of their better-brought-up or environmentally more fortunate classmates. We have also found that students who fail to do well scholastically often compensate by seeking attention as bullies; and when these are segregated into classes on the basis of academic scores, the resulting concentration of hard cases compounds disciplinary problems. RPL avoids this through heterogeneous grouping.

Desegragation of the Camden schools began in earnest in 1970. During this period, the high school more than doubled its number of black students almost overnight. Many of the students came from the lowest economic stratum, creating a volatile situation not only racially but also socially. Yet there have been no serious outbreaks of violence attributable to racial intolerance. Violence of other origin has been minimal, and we can state confidently that our school has been free of the kind of turmoil that elsewhere has well-nigh ground education to a halt. We believe that RPL has contributed to this comparative harmony. Mr. Clyde Jones, assistant principal of Camden High School and a former biology teacher, wrote in a critique of the Ramseur System, "One of the complaints of the black students since the total integration of our schools is that their grades are lower now than before. Many of them attribute this to discrimination. We have received no complaints from black students in RPL, for they make their choice and their work can be reviewed." Also, Mr. William D. Chivers, assistant principal of Camden High School and assistant principal of the former all black Jackson High School in Camden, stated in a taped interview, "RPL has helped cut discipline problems to a minimum."

As for pruning out dead faculty wood, we have already shown how RPL provides a fair, consistent, and realistic basis for judging a teacher's performance. In fact, without RPL, how does a principal nowadays clear his staff of an incompetent teacher? He may know she is dreadful. The faculty and students may know. The entire community may be aware of that teacher's gross lack of ability. But without RPL, how is it to be proved with objective conclusiveness?

Ramseur System records provide the evidence justifying dismissal—evidence that cannot be refuted or rejected on any grounds, including those charges of discrimination that can liquify the knees of the most redoubtable administrator.

But what RPL cannot do is convert a sow's ear into a silk purse.

We fully sympathize with the delicate position of principals, their exhausting day, and the sometimes insoluble problems on every level with which they have to deal and for which we can offer no remedy. On the other hand, there are those who create their problems. Difficult as the job may be, it can be handled if the right person is chosen. We can affirm this from our experience of blessed memory with one "head" whose superb leadership helped him avoid the ambushes that strew the paths of so many administrators. Many principals, we regret to say, are equipped neither intellectually nor temperamentally, nor by acquired experience, for the position. An increasing number are political appointees whose qualifications are less than self-evident and who, in short order, prove that, in fact, they have none.

Our man was different.

First, he had been respected as a teacher. His degree and experience were in the academic field. Except in the rarest of cases, that's the only background that can qualify someone for the post of principal. Having been a teacher, our man understood that the imparting of knowledge is a school's chief function; in fact, its only *raison d'être*. A school was not a holding pen for delinquents. It was not a thrill-a-second rollercoaster ride. It was not a muscle factory dedicated to the production of championship tiddlywink teams. He had coached briefly, and as a teacher and administrator, he obviously enjoyed sports and supported athletic programs enthusiastically. But he never put athletics ahead of academic or vocational needs. That was the first thing about this rare person.

Second, he possessed sensitivity. He never implemented any new idea without discussing it with the faculty and gaining their approval. His interest was in the welfare of students and teachers, not in adding to his professional resumé. He never purchased materials or made decisions for departments without first consulting the members of that department. They were treated as experts in their field. He backed all his teachers in the disciplinary actions they took. If he disagreed with their decisions, he would discuss it with them and advise them, but he realized they were on the front line and had to speak with the voice of authority if the school were to run smoothly.

Third, he had absolute integrity. He made his views known to the faculty. He laid down clean lines of responsibility. Any new policy or any assignment of classes, subjects, or positions was clearly defined as his or someone else's decision. There was no "buck-passing" in his school.

Fourth, he had no illusions about his infallibility, and he had the grace, sense, and humility to admit mistakes. He was not afraid to back away from a bad decision, and he did not feel that it was beneath his dignity to seek advice. He had the courage to do so, too. If he did not have a ready answer for some thorny problem, he would take council with his teachers.

He was, in short, a most amazing person, an exception, as principals go. Would you believe it?—he treated his faculty as professionals, and he expected them to act that way. He was not a despot who felt he had to keep his staff "in place," preaching sermons about love of and dedication to youth while treating the faculty as though they were cretins. On the contrary, he showed respect for everyone, teacher or student. Guess what he got in return?

He was no Mr. Milquetoast, don't get us wrong. But he was unfailingly considerate and ever mindful that we all have our dignity, even when we've slipped up. If, on occasion, a faculty member needed reprimanding, that teacher was called in for a private talk. Students were the object of the same consideration. In the privacy of his office, after listening to whatever defense teacher or student might summon on his behalf, he could come down like a ton of bricks, confirming his authority; but during such a session he always emphasized the teacher's (or student's) capabilities, encouraging him to do his best. Rarely did these meetings end with any bitterness or ill-will.

We are speaking, of course, about a person whose

rare humility of spirit disdained any show of power and the afflatus that balloons so many principals. He never summoned the faculty to the conference room for the sake of it—there had to be a purpose. We were not forced into being a captive audience for any insurance or book salesman pushing a product, nor for exhaustive reviews of educational programs that long and bitter experience had shown us did not contribute to the quality of the curriculum. No convocation was ever held to give his faculty a "raking over." We remember an incident in a nearby school where the principal was known to vent his moods in large assemblies. The beginning of one school year found him in a particularly bad humor, so he read the riot act to his teachers, promising all kind and degree of dire penalties if they did not shape up for the coming term. After the meeting, one bewildered young teacher walked out in a daze, asking in a frightened voice, "What could I have done? I got here just today."

Among the other virtues of our paragon, he never showed partiality. He could not have liked all of his teachers equally, but his preferences were unknown. He did not discuss personalities with his staff. He was friendly to his faculty and students but never overly familiar. He was, nonetheless, loyal. He was the liaison officer for his teachers at the central office (superintendents, supervisors, and board members), and he fought for them when he felt they were justified in a grievance.

The secret of his success was in his concept of what a principal should be. In his own words, "My job is to work for the teachers. They are the educators. My duty is to provide the materials and atmosphere they need. I give the orders only when they do not or cannot perform effectively."

Why aren't more principals cut from this cloth? What are the qualifications for the position? On what basis are principals chosen? The only standard requirement is a master's degree in administration. Until recently, the field was usually narrowed to available male teachers, the majority having been originally hired to fill some opening in the coaching staff. Such ridiculous practice is indefensible, unless it is asuumed that we teachers are so fearsome a lot that a bull-neck and 200 pounds of gristle are required to keep us in order. A coaching background *plus scholastic credentials* does not *preclude* administrative ability, but the very nature of a coach's job demands an almost exclusive dedication to physical training. Although most coaches are assigned academic courses to teach, their hours are so absorbed by the sport that they can spare little time preparing and evaluating class work. They are paid, remember, for winning games, not academic scholarships.

I, Nancy, know. I coached tennis for six years. I enjoyed every minute of it and remember the time with pleasure. I also admit that my history students were often short-changed academically. They did not complain. They probably enjoyed the in-season reprieve from some of my demands in off-season time. Meanwhile, the hours devoted to practice and to home and out-of-town matches blasted my afternoons; on occasion, even a portion of the school day. I continued to coach for one year after RPL was adopted by the school, but soon realized that the two simply could not mix. Reluctantly—and I mean reluctantly—I gave up the tennis. The academic and athletic disciplines *cannot* be mixed, and those administrators whose primary background is athletics are poorly attuned to the scholastic situation and tend, often, to try to run schools as though they were fielding a track team. What we're saying is that principals should be selected from the academic staff. With this as the first premise, RPL becomes once again invaluable.

An RPL teacher knows his stuff—records prove it. He has the skills to teach and evaluate young people—records, again, prove it. They also reveal that he can work with and discipline his students; otherwise, he would not be able to impart his knowledge to a class. A good teacher may not possess the managerial talents to make a good principal. A poor teacher *definitely* will not make one.

A principal is in the public eye. He is a salesman for his school and public education. He must be able to convey to his community local educational needs. He must, therefore, as a least qualification, speak decent English. It is helpful if he can distinguish between like and as and good and well.

One principal of whom we have vivid recollection mounted the stage to give his students a rousing speech on patriotism. "There never was," he thundered, "a *more better* man than Benjamin Franklin." Another principal of vivid recollection insisted on getting back into the classroom occasionally to expound at length on the importance of the *Noble* Peace prize. He was also given to walking down the school corridors, twirling an umbrella and saying to anyone who passed him by, "Look what I con-fit-e-cated!" We have had the privilege of the acquaintance of a supervisor, no less, who delivered the first speech of the year to the faculties of the area, several hundred teachers. He obviously enjoyed his profound statements, which he delivered in orotund tones. He will never know how profound their effect was. He began with the usual flattery and enthusiasm that are fed to teachers as a starter for a new term. Then he began to admonish them about their duties, threatening awful consequences. After each of his points, he would pause, lean over the lectern, and say in a deep, dramatic voice, "... and if you do not do right, the lights will go out, and there shall be such darkness!" What lights and what kind of darkness were not clear to us, nor was it clear how he himself, our leader, planned to escape the apocalypse in the making of which he participated. The speech came to an end with pious exhortations to love and fellowship, culminating with his promise that if we all did our duty, we would—a pause; hand crashing down on the lectern—"CAP THE GAMOOT!"

RPL can't cap every gamoot, but it helps.

Chapter XII
The Student: Tomorrow's Hope

The young person of today compared with the one of a generation ago • RPL's influence on students' attitudes: their view of honesty, their apathy, their complaints about school policy • Their attitudes the result of their training: lax discipline and neglect of adults in supplying guidelines • The teachers' role

Have we unaccountably spawned a generation of monsters? Have we reared a hatch of drifters, rip-off artists, and bums?

Are young people *really* different from those of a generation ago? On gloomy days when low cash balances, unpaid bills, and our children's depressed standing for the semester all look like a statement of fiscal and mental bankruptcy, they seem to be.

Mr. Cotter was exasperated. "John, you are going to get a zero for cheating on this test, and, if it happens again, you will be dismissed from the class and receive an "F" for the course." But John yawned, "Why me? Most everybody cheats. It's no big deal. What about the others?"

Mr. Cotter told him firmly, "If I catch them, they will receive the same treatment. Now, would you like to tell me who else cheated on the test?"

John came alive at this. "Of course not! That wouldn't be very honorable."

The young are *not* all that different from past generations. Given a chance, they retain an acute sense of justice and fairness. We will always remember the words of one of our students who responded indignantly to our annual, start-of-the-year lecture on honesty. He jumped to his feet and told us that he was tired of hearing about the evils of cheating from the biggest deceivers of all—teachers! He rushed on to say that he and his friends resented the passing grades that are handed out to students who in no way merit them, and that none of them, besides, appreciated or understood how that could be either rationalized as compassion or justified as a reward for so-called effort.

He was difficult to answer.

When deception is endemic in any system, it takes an unusually mature young person to distinguish between the moral wrongs sometimes masked by hypocrisy that he sees perpetrated everywhere around him, and his obligation, notwithstanding, to do right. Some students excuse their dishonesty by accusing teachers of setting standards too high; others condemn scheduling for placing them in too advanced a class. Also, parents who, in return for such privileges as use of the family car, demand good grades, irrespective of how they are earned, share the blame.

Not all parents are oblivious to the bales of shoddy that are being sold as diplomas. Columnist William Raspberry wrote in August of 1978:

> . . . I . . . hear from . . . parents whose children [they believe] . . . are learning far less than they could be learning . . . And they believe it with good reason. These children make good grades—above-average grades—while playing their way through school.
>
> "You reporters are forever writing about the children who aren't motivated, who are discipline problems, who finish high school as functional illiterates," one father

told me recently. "Well, I guess you could say my son is motivated. He certainly can read and do math. He's getting good grades, but he's not doing a damned thing. He's just sliding through."

This man is thinking of putting his son in private school.

I get the same sort of complaints from parents who write to me from across the country . . .

The complaint is not that the children are bombing out or that they will have trouble finding decent jobs or getting into college. The complaint is that they are not being "stretched." They are perfectly willing to work hard at school, but they don't have to. Their grades come too easily.[1]

Nobody wants shoddy. As well as parents, more children than one would think, desire rewards commensurate with their achievement. They do not like being bilked, and when they feel that the education they are getting is a cheat as well as a delusion, they become cynical, resentful, and contemptuous. They take their standards of honor from their elders, and they give back in kind.

RPL can help modify students' attitudes about honesty by eliminating some of the glib excuses that today sanction personal irresponsibility and by providing a challenge that restores pride in a job well-done. The student himself elects the degree of difficulty that he feels he can handle. Neither his schedule nor his teacher will determine that for him. Through its division of students into groups suited to their ability, RPL helps to avert the pressure of ambitious parents for top grades that their child, perhaps, can never achieve when an absolute standard is set for all. The parent is intimately involved with the child's choice of group and becomes supportive instead of negatively demanding. And when a teacher can deal with children at levels on which they are able to perform, he does not feel the temptation to fudge reality by gift-wrapping specious passes for those unhappy youngsters who seem to try so hard yet continue to flunk. Even the minor, procedural detail, that differently designed tests are given to the three groups and that no homogeneous seating arrangement is prescribed, reduces the chances of cheating.

Mrs. Evans, a guidance counselor, was a good soul. Robin worried her. Thought of Robin upset her no matter how much Geritol she took. "What has happened to you?" she pleaded with him one afternoon. "Your grades have fallen steadily, and this is your senior year!"

Robin was a worse case than John by far. To his congenital mononucleosis, which seemed to sap all his mental energy, he added spastic twitching of feet during the first ten minutes of class, a glazed stare, and an apparently incurable case of narcolepsy before the quarter hour struck.

He told her, "Bored, I guess. The classes are dull and the teachers spend half the time reading out of the text or working with 'gooney birds' who still can't get it. But I'll betcha one thing! They'll all pass with a 70, and that means I'll make at least 80 whether I grind or not."

"Aren't you missing the point?" Mrs. Evans protested. "What about college, and after that?"

He was a bright boy, she knew. As a freshman four years back he had shown that he had ability. He had been eager, serious, responsive. She had become very fond of him, and it distressed her more than words to see anomie grow on him year after year. His reply nearly killed her. "I'm not so sure," he said, "that I want college—and what about 'after that'? Why should I give up the fun years of my life poring over books and then work my head off when I get out of school. The 'goonies' will still be getting their 70s when we're at the same factory."

Apathy isn't a congenital disease. It is an acquired attitude, and in students it is a serious deterrent to their educational growth. We're afraid that too many children learn to be apathetic because of the excuse for an education that they are getting, which also twists their sense of what is right. Resentful as they can be of the unearned passing grades lavished on so many of their fellows, they, nevertheless, like Robin, view their own unearned 80s and 90s as a "right." Thus, students float through school without academic effort, gaining little or no knowledge, but cultivating along the way a growing bitterness for their less fortunate peers, for educators—for society in general. They are bored as can be with their intermediate status as students, and they are as apparently unconcerned as they are in reality apprehensive about their future.

The Ramseur System doesn't *give* grades; it *records* the grade that the child earned and the level of his success. It recognizes—say, even honors—failure; and the Robins of this world soon discover that a "cool" pose of indifference is, under RPL, self-defeating. It brings a zero sure as Judgment Day. On the happy side, RPL students quickly adapt to a system under which, whereas laziness is disdained, achievement gets its just reward. Is it too much for us to claim that the more children who are trained under the Ramseur System, the more enthusiastic, determined, and industrious adults will we have in our society tomorrow? We think not.

A local survey that examined 240 students randomly chosen from ninth, tenth, eleventh, and twelfth grade classes in Camden High School confirmed what our years of personal contact always led us to suspect: most of the traumas developed by young people about their education are natural to that time in life when the adolescent is struggling with the transition from childhood to adulthood under a system that is basically flawed and whose coddling of false values does everything except help them. We can't pretend that RPL, all by itself, will revolutionize the contemporary ethos of unreality, but some of the minor yet important legitimate complaints that this study singles out can be wholly avoided under our way of education.

1. As a general rule, it was found, students resent being placed in classes that categorize them as slow or "dumb." *RPL students place and label themselves.*

2. A second finding was that students do not like to be forced to conform to adult decisions about their life; they like to have a part in forming their own image. *RPL students, by choice of group work, themselves decide on what their ambitions will be and accept the responsibility for that choice. RPL students, moreover, help to design their work. They in fact create their own image.*

3. Students resent grades that do not clearly define their achievement. *RPL grades profile precisely what degree of skill has been acquired.*

4. Students resent "busy work." *So do we, and we don't allow it. All assignments must have a purpose. All work will be graded.*

5. Students (understandably) fear grading that

may be based on a teacher's disapproval. *RPL removes the influence of personal feelings. Students are protected by the teacher's annotations, which determine what mark he gets. Those grades are clearly defined for the different levels, and each student controls his own evaluation.*

6. Students resent being maneuvered into subjects merely to acquire showcase marks, rather than being allowed to pursue what they believe will be useful to them in the future. *No such pressure is put on RPL students. They can take the courses they want in the group they choose with no fear of being judged by grades alone. The RANK in which the grade is achieved is clearly reflected on the records.*

7. Students mature at different ages and for different reasons and do not wish to be bound to a given level because of past performance alone. *At the moment an RPL student is inspired or prepared to move to a higher group, he may, for he is never held to a less demanding level for an entire year unless he chooses to remain there.*

If young people today are basically the same as they were in the past; if their dreams are the same, and if they strain at the bonds of youth as others did before them and others to come surely always will, fighting discipline imposed from on high as they struggle to discipline themselves; and if there is no *biological* difference between Peck's Bad Boy of yore, Huckleberry Finn, and our young Robin, who is getting nowhere and going nowhere; then what has made the difference in general attitude from that of past generations? We conclude that the deterioration in student behavior today, apart from everything else that may contribute to it, is a consequence of adults having abandoned the training of young people. Certainly it must be frightening to approach maturity without any guidelines and without the help of someone older and wiser.

The student in secondary education, when you come to think of it, has had very little youth. He has been reared by books on childhood and adolescent psychology that, by stressing rationalizations for his behavior, have encouraged acceptance of all forms of conduct. Court decisions[2] have endowed him with adult privileges while protecting him from adult responsibilities. He has grown up playing grown-up without the emotional maturity or experience to understand the possible consequences of his choices and actions. The rules that govern his behavior are improvised to justify his desires of the moment. The rules change as his whims change.

This generation of parents has indulged, excused, pampered, and flattered the child, and, naturally, he has happily accepted the attention. He has been told by educators, psychologists, his mother, father, or guardian, and, of course—always—politicians that he is a member of the "smartest generation this world has ever seen," with the implicit corollary that everybody owes this genius something and he owes nothing to anyone. We've alluded to this before. Everybody involved in the business of education is grabbing for every device on the market to keep the child happy and to see that he is filled with glee every moment of each school day of his life. The more bored he becomes, the more overtures are made to lift his spirits and entice him to learn. If he refuses to take the first step himself toward education, education of some sort will be brought to him. He knows he will graduate whether he

deserves to or not. He has little respect for those who
teach him. He doesn't believe they know their stuff.
Also, he believes teachers and administrators are
afraid—afraid to discipline students; afraid to fail students; afraid to speak out against policies that are
detrimental to education. He's right. And in their fear,
they shrink from placing any restraints on the business of growing up.

Parents, even more so than teachers, have neglected
to supply the guidelines that young people necessarily
must have if they are to be protected from their own
follies and allowed to be young. The tragedy isn't fully
realized until those children have to cope with tomorrow. The present love affair with youth is evident
wherever one turns. Advertisements appeal to the
young; adults mimic them in manner and, frequently,
in dress, whereas once the adult was the model for the
child. Don't think this took place only in the preposterous 1960s. Three thousand years ago Theopompus
stated, "An unseemly fascination with youth is the
surest sign of old age." Plato declared that when older
men, scholars, and rulers, ". . . adopt the manners of
the young . . . such is the fair and glorious beginning
out of which springs tyranny." Plato was speaking
politically, which isn't our concern, but we do know
about the tyranny that many children exercise over
their mothers and fathers. Hoping to understand little
Johnny better, parents have attempted to bridge the
"generation gap" by abdicating the parental role for
the "pal" role. Their "understanding" of the child is
often reflected in excuses for him. For example: a
school has a rule that absences are accepted as valid
only in cases of a child's illness, or illness or death in
the immediate family. But Frankie has not completed

an assignment that is due the following day. If the work is not in on time he will receive an "F." *Understandably,* he is in a predicament. Does he go to school and receive an "F" for incomplete work or does he stay out to finish his assignment and receive punishment for an unexcused absence? Daddy writes a note stating that he was sick on that day. Frankie returns to school with the excuse in one hand and his completed paper in the other. This is an act of disrespect for school rules, teachers, and administrators—and also will lead to a lack of respect on the part of Frankie for his father.

Lax discipline inevitably engenders disrespect. Parents are primarily responsible because discipline begins at home. Schools cannot be expected to discharge a responsibility that the parents have abdicated. In concert, parents, educators, and the judicial system have fostered the deplored attitudes of the young by insisting that the student should not be molded to fit society but that, instead, society should conform to the desires of the student. If this viewpoint on rearing and educating children had dominated history, man would still be trying to move out of the cave. For this philosophy to *succeed,* one should be born old and die young. When adulthood becomes a shameful, degrading, and despised state, then no one will be able to accept age; and eventually everyone will have worked his way back to the playpen, where all society can happily beat its baby rattles against the rails.

What can teachers do? We can give our young an educational system that exalts honor, respect, ambition, and justice. RPL does this. It makes acts of dishonesty difficult to commit and unacceptable to teachers and students. It insists on abidance by the rules. It is equitable in itself, and it instills in the

student an understanding of reality by admitting failure while making success possible. Let's give the student a fair chance to become an educated man. He is
what this book is all about—he is the reason for the
Ramseur System. We are interested in his dreams and
ideas, and we are, obviously, concerned for his tomor-
rows. His future is, after all, ours also. It is a road we
will travel together.

Footnotes, Chapter XII

[1] William Raspberry, "Students 'Slide By' In School," *The State*
(Newspaper, Columbia, S. C.), August 29, 1978.

Chapter XIII
Parents: Guardians of Tomorrow

*The significance of the parent as initiator of reform
• Influence of home environment • The confused
roles of the home and the school in the training of
the young • The parents' concerns: importance of
child's scholastic success, fear of assignment of child
to special class, confusion about school programs,
poor relationship with teachers • RPL's restoration of
parental role • Appeal for parental reassessment
of values*

Although we write in order to help fellow teachers
restore integrity to the schools, our appeal is ultimately addressed to parents. *Without parental insistence on better education there will be none.*

We all know that there is an educational malaise of
epidemic proportions. and it's tempting to despair; but
despair is the capital sin. We *can* do something about
it: as ordinary individuals, as mothers and fathers of
children who are being culturally deprived. Take on
the whole mess? No. Obviously not. Educational ills
are being addressed on a national scale all the time—
poorly, ineffectively, mistakenly—without regard to
specific regional needs. The application in Houston of a
remedy that seemed to help in Albany may provoke a
new crisis. Even within a county the dilemmas of one
school can be quite different from those of another.

The reformer's approach has to be more modest. To

oxygenate our educational system as a whole we must turn our attention to the individual patient—the local school. Here parents can take the initiative in reform. They know what kind of education their children are getting, the quality of the teachers, the ability of the principal. (Or, if they don't, they ought to and can find out.) In their community, parents have political clout. They can—if they will—handle something close to them, something they can observe, something they can comprehend. They need not sink like Silly Putty into discouraged heaps because of the seemingly insurmountable problems of the entire country. Administer to the patient at hand and it will naturally follow that the condition of our public schools across the land will be at least improved.

Rescue operations for education, therefore, like the proper rearing of children, begin at home. We mean this in a literal sense as well; and here we speak to parents directly. The pre-grammar school child himself must be better and more conscientiously reared, because everything reduces to a matter of true values, and the values with which young children are imbued by their mothers and fathers carry forward in the school environment. If our public schools are engaged in educational chicanery, selling shoddy for true worth, is it not at least partly because the contemporary American family has adopted false values? We go back to the abdication of the parental role we touched upon in the preceding chapter.

The first seven years of a child's life are morally formative years. If parents have not taught children right conduct, respect, honesty, and the other hoary virtues by that time, how can the schools be expected to do so after the critical period of incubation has gone by? Public schools have had dumped on them too many of the responsibilities of rearing children, to the degree that teachers have been driven loco *in loco parentis.* In fact, tending to the child's intellectual development nowadays often takes second place to nourishing him in health and body and social behavior. Teachers are saddled with supervising youngsters at play, showing them how to use dental floss, explaining the birds and the bees (and watch out, Louise), tending to their emotional problems whether they bear any relation or not to school, and taking over all disciplinary responsibilities because parents *will not do so themselves.* That schools have assumed what formerly was the prerogative, not to say fundamental obligation, of parents seems perfectly acceptable to our society. Obviously, the courts also feel educators are enchanted to take on the job of rehabilitating juvenile offenders, since judges often parole a delinquent child to his parents upon the stipulation that he must attend school. The buried premise is that public schools are handy holding pens for keeping delinquents off the streets, where they are routinely expected to commit more crimes. Splendid: put the little thug in school, where his potential victims are plentiful, young, frightened, and defenseless!

As the school's social sway over the child has grown—with tacit consent of those who now object— parents have surrendered more and more control of their child's academic training. Naturally. Bureaucracy hates a vacuum. To put the matter bluntly, the selfishness and laziness of too many parents have reduced them to meek acquiescence before whatever edict the School Board or some state or federal agency may dictate. They may not select the school their child will attend, indeed not, for he will be assigned to whatever given PHS bureaucrats please. They may not select the type of program under which their child will strive to become a civilized human being, for available federal money is often the determining factor in the adoption of a local plan. They may not choose the fields of study their young will enter, for the mandatory ones are decided by administrators at state level. Parents *do* have some say in the child's selection of courses, so long as the number of units required for the different fields of academic study are completed; however, selection of teachers and level of difficulty *within* the class are beyond their control. Naturally, conscientious parents are frustrated, but they do not know where to turn. The understanding and support of these parents are essential to the proper functioning of any program, yet most contacts with teachers take place at P.T.A. meetings that tend to be formal and impersonal in nature. Specific days may be set aside for parents' visits to classrooms to observe teaching in action, but since everyone is on his best behavior at such times, the impressions that are carried home are illusionary.

The only contacts between parents and educators in the normal course of events is when either request a conference because of academic or disciplinary problems. These encounters are seldom fruitful. First, they take place when a crisis has already occurred instead of in time to avert it. Then, natural protectiveness inclines people to excuse their child for poor behavior or performance. The school staff is to blame. ("After all, you have him seven and a half hours a day, minimum, every day except weekends and vacations, whereas we're lucky to get a glimpse of him between breakfast and *Mork and Mindy*.") And many parents, confused by ceaseless experiments with new teaching methods, and for excellent reason distrustful of them, judge the merit of any system in the light of how well their child did. This means top marks.

To the average mother and father, scholastic success is all-important, and grades are the sole determinant of that, the only criteria they trust. Parents agonize over whether their child will get into college. The prestige! The rewards! College folk, as everyone knows, climb into the 70% bracket much more surely and quickly than others. (Their divorce and suicide rates are higher, too—but that's beside the point.) Rarely do fond mothers and fathers question their darling's ability to take on that challenge, or wonder whether he has been properly prepared to survive the first cut once he is accepted. (Never mind that many private colleges and state universities themselves foster the ethos of unreality by policies of open admissions and fail-safe grading.) Didn't Alice get straight "A's"? A high mark, regardless of what it may mean or how it was achieved, certifies success; therefore, parental pressure for the symbols of superior performance all too often induces children to seek out subjects most likely to guarantee glistening grades rather than those more exacting courses that will prepare them for higher education. Unrealistic parental ambition (educators are well aware who pays the bills; they are not more heroic than most people) has also inclined many administrators to lean on teachers to mark indulgently. The pandemic consequence is an utter falsification of what students actually learned. But shouldn't we ask: Who in the first place demanded this falsification? Where did the perversion of values begin?

Parents also fear that, because of previous poor performance and the ever awesome and threatening standardized test scores, their child will be incarcerated in some dumb-dumb dungeon, cut off from his friends. This fear has sufficient grounds. For example, a child may be assigned without ill effects to a special class for a number of hours a week to improve his reading, but when he is scheduled into remedial classes for slow students in any of the regular, required courses, there is indeed a good chance that he will be forever handicapped academically and socially.

Parents get upset because all too often they have no idea in the world what precisely their child is supposed to be learning . . . for the good reason that, in the first place, they don't even know what academic discipline their child is studying. This isn't surprising either, when basic cooking is disguised by such an imaginative title as "The History and Mystery of Comestibles," a course in grammar is labelled "Practical Tools," and one on retail sales is given the grandiloquent designation of "Distributive Education." Such euphemisms, testifying to an inexcusable intellectual snobbery on top of intellectual bankruptcy, understandably outrage as well as mystify those who retain some notions about integrity; but parents as a whole have to accept a share in the blame once again, because it is their worship of status that has given rise to these preposterous shams.

Laying aside the question of blame, how can we who spend our professional careers worrying about the children in our charge solicit the support of parents? Too often, teachers think of them as meddlesome busybodies. This, at least, is how *parents* perceive our attitude. It can be true; and speaking as educators

ourselves, how unfortunate that a quasi-adversary relationship has grown between people whose interests
should be identical (the welfare of children) and who
need to collaborate in the educational enterprise more
than ever before. We teachers need parents as allies in
the worst day. If we can get their enthusiastic support,
the battle for integrity in public education is half won.
In the final analysis, they hip the burden through their
taxes; and the defeat of one educational bond issue
after another in recent state elections over the past
decade shows that parents are fed up with costlier and
costlier schools that do not educate. Parents have
legitimate concerns that teachers must set at rest before they can hope to enlist them in the common cause,
because parents cannot otherwise be expected to
understand the school's position. And mutual comprehension is vital.

So what else estranges the natural allies of
teachers? Well, there are four more common complaints on our list. Parents fear reprisal on their children if they manifest a concern that may be taken by
teachers as interference. They resent the invasion of
privacy by the personal data in questionnaires that
their children are obliged to complete. They sometimes suspect teachers of indoctrinating the young in
their personal moral and political philosophies; and,
finally, they object to teachers usurping—as they see
it—*their* role, as though teachers are best-equipped to
plan *their* children's future.

With all these fears, irritations, and suspicious, the
Ramseur System can help. Grading (Chapter V) and
ranking (ChapterVI), for example, clearly define a
student's true academic standing, thus eliminating
unrealistic and harmful pressure for the empty status

symbols of fictitiously high marks. On the other hand, no child under RPL is discriminated against intellectually. Since every class includes different cognitive levels, there is no need to separate slow learners* from the advanced ones; therefore, no test, standardized or otherwise, consigns a child to limbo—RPL students, as we've emphasized a dozen times, place themselves.

The student folder (Chapter III) and the RPL letter remove other worries. We refer to the missive that goes out to parents at the beginning of every school year, explaining the grading system and encouraging them to seek additional information. Parents are also given notice that their child's folder is available at all times for their inspection. (If it is inconvenient to drive to the school in order to review the folder, it can be taken home by the child). Parents do not have to guess what their children are studying. Classes on grammar are called Grammar, and classes on mechanical drawing, or typing, or in the use of the lathe are identified as just what they are, and they're all listed. The folder also reveals whether any information of a personal nature has been recorded, and whether there is evidence of teacher "reprisal" for "interference" by parents. Parents can see for themselves what is written and how their child's papers have been graded.

Regarding ideological indoctrination, RPL cannot prevent some teachers from abusing their position. (Ideologs are everywhere, though we do our best to ferret them out.) Nor is it realistic to expect that teachers, however hard they try, won't in some form reveal their personal positions on sensitive matters.

---

*This does not apply to students with learning disabilities that require special materials and trained personnel to treat their handicaps.

Most teachers try to adhere to a strict objectivity, but discussion of morals, religion, or politics can't be avoided in history, government, civics, literature, and other broad courses in which there is philosophical content.

We have to expand on this. Teachers in non-sectarian public schools commonly uphold the ethics that derive from Judeo-Christian tradition whether or not they practice a religion. But if a child asks a teacher such an explosive question as, "Do you believe in God?"—an answer must be given. The teacher who does not personally accept the existence of a Supreme Being, if he is practical, responsible, experienced, and wise, will reply in this manner: "I don't happen to believe in such a Being, but hundreds of millions of people all over the world do. What anyone believes is the result of his personal experience, upbringing, temperament, and many other factors. I do think that all of us should learn the different concepts people have about the existence of God, because a person's religious philosophy can be the motivating force in how he works, plays, brings up children, lives, and, yes, how he dies." That may sound like a mealy-mouthed evasion, but a teacher must be candid about her personal beliefs while at the same time taking scrupulous care not to be offensive and in no way to slur or derogate the beliefs of her charges.

The teacher who *does* believe in a traditional God will say so and give a similar innocuous answer, explaining that, depending on upbringing or intellectual decision after a thorough study of the matter, and so forth, some people ultimately come down on one side or the other; and that an agnostic or atheist can be ethically as observant of right and wrong as the practicing

Christian or Jew.* The obvious criterion that good teachers follow, whether in matters of religion or politics, is that personal beliefs should not be imposed on students and that any subtle attempt to indoctrinate them against the options held by their parents is inexcusable. A test or classroom question that elicits of children their thoughts on these matters should be graded according to their interior logic, not on the basis of the teacher's convictions. Sometimes, as we all know, teachers abuse the ethics of their profession; the Ramseur System offers not total but at least partial protection against such impropriety. By reviewing their child's work folder, parents see at once what has been discussed and whether there is hidden bias in the grading. The folder will reveal if the teacher has violated in any way the canons of teaching—to be honest, responsible, and discreet.

Perhaps the greatest benefit of the student's RPL file and its availability to parents is that this keeps both sides in constant touch with each other. Both are encouraged to contribute in their distinctive way. The following example (Figure 7) shows what we mean.

Mark Matthews stayed all year in Group 2, though he failed repeatedly to meet the requirements for that level. Each reporting period his teacher, Miss Grey, wrote an explanation of the "U" ("U" stands for unsatisfactory work in Levels 1 and 2) and requested a conference with his parents to discuss Mark's problems. She also reminded them that "U" work in Groups 1 and 2 would have to be recorded on the permanent record as a failing grade for the course if a student did

* We may personally think this proposition false except in special cases, but the myths of the secular state have to be upheld in schools supported by the state.

Figure 7

SUBJECT __Spanish II__   YEAR _____
STUDENT'S NAME __Matthews, Mark__   GROUP I __60__
SUBJECT TEACHER __C. Cherry__   GROUP II __80__
HOMEROOM TEACHER __M. Smith__   GROUP III __96__

1st 6 weeks		Grade	Group
Comments	62	U	2

2nd 6 weeks			
Comments	60	U	2

3rd 6 weeks			
Comments	53	U	2
1st Sem. Exam.	58		2
1st Sem. Average	59		2

4th 6 weeks			
Comments	45	U	2

5th 6 weeks			
Comments	51	U	2

6th 6 weeks			
Comments	42	U	2
2nd Sem. Exam.	43		2
2nd Sem. Average	46		2

Pilot Light Form 2 Year   Grade __53__   Group __2__ not transfer to a group that he could handle. In Mark's case, not until the end of the *fifth reporting period* was there any response. Miss Grey received a note from Mark's father, who wrote,

> We appreciate your concern and apologize for our delay in contacting you. Mark has been a problem to us this year and has fought a battle with his mother and me over his right to the family car, week-end vacations, and other privileges. We have refused him these privileges because he has failed to study and earn these special pleasures. I guess he thinks he is punishing us by refusing to do those things that would please us. We feel he is quite capable of doing Group 2 work, and we have refused to accept Group 3 level from him. Thank you again for your interest and concern.

In our opinion, Mark's parents were bullheaded and made a very great mistake; nevertheless, it is for them to decide for their son, not teachers, not administrators, and certainly not the state; it is parents who must shoulder the degree of responsibility that they feel proper. If they believe their child is capable of deciding for himself and want him to exercise that responsibility, RPL allows the parent—not the teacher, not the administrator—to insist that this be done. If, on the other hand (as in Mark's case), parents believe their child is *not* capable of electing his workload, then they must abide by the consequences. The parent, better than the teacher, can judge the actual effort of the child; the teacher judges the results of that effort.

Although the Ramseur System cannot force parents to take an active interest in their child's education, it insistently encourages it, and RPL places the responsibility where it should be—on the mother and father, whether they care to accept it or not. Local schools reflect the values of the adult population, and this is where our educational problems begin. Educators naturally tend to promote those values that the American public seems to regard above all others—prestige and money. (Recent strikes by some public school teachers unfortunately suggest that they themselves participate in the worship of mammon that most are so quick to deplore.) A high school diploma will assure a young person $5,000 more a year than a student with no diploma, and a college degree is worth $10,000 more, or so the propaganda goes. A successful child is one who has officially acquired the status of an educated person and can prove it with his diploma first and bank book second, and never mind how he got both. No one seems to question whether his diploma attests to anything at all and whether he would have been a better, happier, and more productive person in some less lucrative field. He too, probably, will never doubt his choice, for he has been inculcated with the idea since earliest childhood that success is material.

Jerry and Bob, twin brothers, are tragic examples. Neither was a good student. They were from a poor but proud family. Jerry, blustery and defensive, was very protective of Bob, who had physical as well as mental handicaps. Jerry became fond of his history teacher, Mrs. Reese, in whom he had complete trust. He had stretched the school rules many times and was constantly being ushered to the principal's office because he could not control his temper. One day he went too far, calling a teacher an s.o.b. In those days, expulsion was still an expedient that principals used when the offense warranted it. Before leaving the building for the last time, Jerry paid a visit to Mrs. Reese. He asked her to take care of Bob, who, he said, would be lost for a while without his protection. She promised to help in any way she could. Bob could not write his name legibly, but he had a marvelous gift. He loved any creature, whether it flew, crawled, or walked; wild animals were docile in his hands. He had built a pen where he kept the wounded animals he found on his afternoon walks in the woods behind his home. He nursed them back to health and then returned them to their habitat in the forest. One day Mrs. Reese received a letter from Jerry, who had joined the armed forces, thanking her for looking after Bob and asking for one more favor: ". . . please make Bob study hard so he can go to college and be somebody."

Jerry, who so loved his brother, did not understand. Plato said that a *just* society could exist only if *men* were just, and a just man was one who was in the right place doing that which he was best fitted to do. Aristotle, who is credited as the founder of "liberal" education, said that it must serve the use of leisure in the pursuit of (moral) excellence. We're not obliged to concur with these or any other *apercus,* invested as they may be with the most ancient credentials; but when Plato and Aristotle agree that the primary purpose of education is to produce good men, there's sufficient cause to sit up and take notice. How far we have strayed from that classical concept of what education is truly all about. Bob is less than a man if he does not go to college. He is the victim not of his mental handicaps but of the intellectual snobbery that ordains every student a certified scholar.

This is why so many diplomas have been so disgracefully cheapened. We feel it is undemocratic unless every child at infancy is guaranteed a college

degree as well as the franchise. What a mistaken
fetish for a democracy, whose success depends more on
the moral than the intellectual man. Indeed, as the
late Patrick Lord Devlin—the great British jurist—
pointed out more than a decade age when speaking of
the law's reliance on the "twelve good men and true"
of the jury system, "I am not repelled by . . . submission
to the mentality of the common man. Those who believe in God and that He made Man in His image will
believe also that He gave to each in equal measure the
knowledge of good and evil, placing it not in the intellect wherein his grant to some was more bountiful
than to others, but in the heart and understanding,
building there in each man the temple of the Holy
Ghost. Those who may not believe in God must ask
themselves what they *mean* when they say that they
believe in democracy. Not that all men are born with
equal brains—we cannot believe that; but that they
have at their command the faculty of telling right from
wrong. This is the whole meaning of democracy, for if
in this endowment men were not equal, it would be
pernicious that in the government of any society they
should have equal rights." Without intending to enter
into arguments over the Judeo-Christian foundation
of our republic, Lord Devlin's insight strikes us not
only as true but also as a welcome restatement of
age-old wisdom; not that we, 20th century Americans,
are unique in our misunderstanding of what counts
most in a human being. Back in the 16th century,
Montaigne complained in one of his essays, "In plain
truth, the cares and expense our parents are at in our
education, point at nothing but to furnish our heads
with knowledge; but not a word of judgment and virtue. Cry out, of one that passes by, to the people: 'O,

what a learned man!' and of another, 'O, what a good man!' They will not fail to turn their eyes and address their respect to the former. There should be a third crier, 'O, the blockheads!' "

"Four hundred years later," a friend of ours asks, "have we improved on the vulgarity of perception that elicited Montaigne's disgust? Aren't we still blockheads, laboring under that inversion of values that places the intellectual man first and the moral man second? The capacity, morally and intellectually, to distinguish good from evil, the false from the true, is the essential wisdom. '. . . in truth,' observes Montaigne, 'knowledge is not so absolutely necessary as judgment; the last may make shift without the other but the other never without this.' "[1]

Judgment is a property of the moral being. Education will improve when parents insist on it; but no programmatic approach, not even the Ramseur System, though it does help, will suffice until parents examine their values and rear their children accordingly.

Footnotes, Chapter XIII

[1] Quoted in a lecture, "Education for What?" delivered by Fergus Reid Buckley to the New Jersey Board Association, Atlantic City, N.J., October 26, 1978.

Chapter **XIV**
Discipline: Threats to Tomorrow

Paralysis of purpose of school because of lack of discipline • Appalling figures of rising crime in public schools • Disruption from less grave cases •Demoralizing effect on students and teachers •Causes for break-down in discipline: change in size and make-up of population of schools, method of integration, reaction of blacks and whites to this method, problems in leadership of school, weakness of administrators and teachers in discipline, contribution to turmoil by government interference in schools and by public apathy • Need to reverse directions • An immediate deterrent to lax discipline •Benefits of this method

No system of education, regardless of its merits, can function when the schools are paralyzed by a phenomenon that makes any kind of instruction wellnigh impossible. Literature, math, government—all conventional subjects—are being superseded by an unlisted course whose theme is that crime pays. Rudeness, extortion, defiance of rules, threats, and chilling violence are not only cravenly tolerated by administrators but enhance the offending student's prestige. The crewcut BMOC of the early 1950's has been replaced by juvenile gangsters whose immunity to punishment exalts them in the eyes of their peers, setting—naturally—the most atrocious example. From the microsociety of the school yard, a deplorable tone is sounded for society as a whole; children, far from being civilized in school, are learning from their school experience that the world is a huge dispensing machine for barbarians to rip-off with just that requisite brutality, cunning and effrontery necessary to terrorize the law-abiding and escape consequences. If nothing is done about the breakdown of discipline, public education had just as well close shop. Perhaps, for the good of the country, it should be abolished.

The appalling figures on rising crime in public schools that are cited almost weekly in national news magazines and in such accounts as Senator Birch Bayh's report to the United States Senate Committee on the Judiciary have availed nothing better than those time-consuming studies that are bureaucrats' last resort when they have no idea what the answer is. All they tell you is that the anarchy and chaos are getting worse all the time, and no longer as a feature of inner city schools alone; crime has spread into every high school of this nation. It has percolated down to grammar schools, where drug usage, vandalism, and theft are no longer uncommon.

Meanwhile—incredibly—a *decrease* in the number of school suspensions is proclaimed by educational authorities. Of course, that there are fewer suspensions doesn't mean that there are fewer outrages, only that they are going unpunished. When a superintendent reassures the board and parents that everything is fine and dandy, and getting dandier by the minute, students and teachers often wonder whether he is talking about the same place they know between the hours of 8 a.m. and 3 p.m. every week. Does he mean that there was no more vandalism today than yesterday? Was there less bullying, or were there fewer muggings, fist fights, and sexual harrassments? Battle-weary teachers ask themselves whether his statement is an effort to convince those who pay him that he is doing a good job, or whether he is merely trying to gloss what he has convinced himself is an insoluble problem. It is possible—shockingly so—that he has become insensible to the mayhem in his school and accepts it as a way of life.

Senator Bayh's subcommittee found that juvenile crime has increased by 245 percent over the last 13 years, with about half of all the serious crimes committed by people under 21. In Brooklyn, New York, a science teacher was hospitalized after being severely beaten by a group of teenage boys. In Los Angeles, a gang of high school girls set fire to a teacher's hair because they were "dissatisfied" with their low marks. Orange County, Florida's Classroom Teachers' Association, reported that in a single year 100 teachers had been assaulted and another 290 had suffered property damage. No wonder appalled commentators conclude not only that "some of our teachers are safer in a dark alley than they are in their classrooms," but also that "children are safer on dark streets than they are in the school hallways and grounds." They hardly exaggerate. The incidence of violence in schools has more than tripled in the last decade. More than 70,000 teachers are physically assaulted every year in classrooms and hallways. The National Education Association has estimated that the annual cost of vandalism would supply books for all public school children in the entire nation. When even the highest educational bureaucracy confesses how grave the situation is from the point of view of administrators, what must students endure? And teachers? Do you remember the *Blackboard Jungle*?

But what about the child, our first concern? Can he feel secure in a setting where rigid government edicts and court decisions protect the wrongdoer more often than the victim? We refer to such legislation as Public Law 94–142, Education of Handicapped Children, whose effect is to make the civil rights of the young, as conceived by obsessed ideologs, the supreme criterion. A disruptive student is allowed to continue to attend classes, regardless of the effect of his behavior on the other children, because he is not to be denied *his* right to an education. This protection has been taken to unbelievable extremes. We know of a nine year old boy who was expelled from school after attempting to force two students (one a boy, the other a girl) into a sexual act with him. These were not his first offenses of a similar nature. But under Public Law 94–142 he has been defined as "emotionally handicapped" and therefore cannot be denied an education within a normal school setting. He was readmitted.

There are cases far less grave, but just as deleterious to maintenance of reasonable order. Adam Martin is lounging in the sun behind the gymnasiom when Mr. Benton appears. "Out of class again? Let me see your corridor pass and your I.D." Adam replies, "I don't have a pass and I've lost my I.D." Mr. Benton is irritated. "Young fellow, this is the third time I have had to send you to the office for the same reasons. What did the principal do to you the last time?" Adam shrugs his shoulders and says, "Nothing, except tell me not to do it again." Does he go unrebuked because of weak administrative policy or because he suffers some serious handicaps that excuses him from the ground rules that govern everyone else? Adam, fit or encumbered, must learn to accept school (and society's) norms, or he will continue to disregard those restrictions that are unpleasant to him. And when a minor infraction is ignored, or treated in the same manner as a more serious one, can the classmates be expected to respect school authorities or, for that matter, the law? A three-day suspension may be handed down to the Tom Sawyer who cuts class on a fine spring day. The same sentence may be meted to the young thug who threatens a teacher, or fights, or steals. How does the well-behaved child adjust to this? Are his experiences and knowledge broad enough for him to intuit as a matter of pragmatic policy what and when to protest, or does he learn to accommodate his moral sense? We might ask, is it our intention to raise the children of this country in the same cynical tradition that blights the civic ethics of Mexican youth, who grow up in the expectancy that the police and all other public figures are almost to the man corrupt, and that not to go along with the system is as foolish as it is idealistic? We can't believe that this is what American parents want. No republic can endure when the citizenry has become venal, and the school environment is critical to the formation of that citizenry. As Alexander Pope put it,

> Vice is a monster of so frightful a mien
> That to be hated needs but to be seen;
> Yet seen too oft, familiar with its face,
> We first endure, then pity, then embrace.

We've talked about discipline before implicitly; we've spoken of the obligation of parents. Now we want to grasp the nettle by its stalk, explaining why we believe that certain errors in sociological judgment, as well as organizational blunders and pusillanimous administrators, are responsible. We treat not only of matters that merit recording on police blotters. Schoolyard rapes and murders grab headlines. They don't begin to tell the story.

Miss Ames left her class to correct a student who was yelling at the top of his voice as he sauntered slowly down the corridor. When she asked him to identify himself, he refused to do so. When asked where he was assigned that period, he retorted, "Why don't you mind your own business and get back in your class where you belong?"

Mr. Finch took a hat from a student who refused to remove it indoors. "You lose my hat, and you'll buy me a new one, understand me—*get* me!" screamed the boy.

Banging on all the lockers as he leisurely made his way to some unknown destination, a high school junior stopped at the end of the hallway after Mrs. Swartz had repeatedly called to him to come back. Slowly turning his head from side to side, with eyes fixed on the ceiling he said, "I just might . . . and again I just might not." After a moment's pause—with exaggerated pretense of deliberation—he added, "After *much* thought I have decided I just might not!" And, whooping with laughter, he disappeared down the stairs.

Miss Carter was on her way to class when a tall student who was leaning against the wall in a hallway stepped in front of her and demanded, "You walk around me, woman." When she refused, he threatened her with the promise that he would "get" her. When the principal tracked him down, he was suspended five days for rudeness. The principal was no man to trifle with, understand. But there was a conflict. The provocation took place on a Thursday. That Friday, as he was reminded, the basketball team had an important game, and the boy was a star forward. Should the whole team be punished for the transgression of one of its members? Certainly not. The sentence was therefore set to begin the following Monday. Sunday brought a deep snow and schools were closed down for a week. When classes were again convened, the five "snow days" were counted as fully satisfying the demands of justice. Naturally so. There was another basketball game Monday night.

Mary asked a teacher to advise her. She was frightened because a boy she did not know was trailing her constantly, brushing against her in the crowded hallways, and making suggestive remarks. The teacher, concerned for Mary's welfare, walked behind her one day and saw that it was true. She advised Mary to take her problem to one of the administrators. The boy had many infractions on his record—the girl, none. The Administrator's first remark to Mary, in the boy's presence, was, "What have you said or done to encourage this young fellow?"

One ninth grader made quite a reputation for himself. He struck a female teacher—before at least 1,000 student and teacher witnesses. The occasion was a student council-sponsored pie-throwing contest. He slammed the pie right into her face, following through with the flat of his hand. The teacher had had no previous contact with this student. He was suspended for two weeks. Shortly afterwards, he admitted to spitting on an instructor's desk for the joy of it. He was considered a first offender (apparently, physically assaulting a teacher did not count). The incident was resolved by a conference between the boy and the instructor whose desk set he had spittled over. Time and again, conferences and counseling were resorted to by authorities, to no effect. That same semester, after constant troublemaking in the classroom, he was allowed to drop two courses. That was all. The school in no meaningful way punished or attempted to reform or even modify his antisocial behavior. It was simply brushed under the rug. Only when he gave vent to his viciousness outside school grounds, by brutally beating his mother, were the police brought in, and he was removed to a correctional institution for—guess what?—more counseling. Shortly afterwards, however, he was released back to the same school that had been too fearful to deal energetically with him in the first place; and there he remained until he sought transfer to another institution. Obviously, this young man was pathologically dangerous to others; yet he was never expelled and the repeated "counseling" remediated his conduct not at all. Yet, even had the school demonstrated the most minimal sense and courage in handling him, the outcome would no doubt have been the same: protection under Public Law 94–142. The boy was, obviously, emotionally unbalanced, therefore, HANDICAPPED; and therefore almost impossible to expel except at the cost of protracted bureaucratic and legal struggle.

We have culled these stories from schools we're acquainted with and from personal experiences. Even in placid, rural communities, teachers are exposed to confrontations with students that leave them shaking with rage and fright, and that can so utterly demoralize them that they lose all composure and wonder whether they are qualified to continue in their profession.

A lovely small town in central South Carolina has been officially designated as one of the "Safe Places."[1] In addition to a proud historical heritage, it has beautiful parks, an excellent recreation program for the young, and one of the better school systems in the state. It can still be counted among the best, though it hasn't been immune to the endemic disciplinary problems that have converted others into battlegrounds. Once, a brief span of time ago, the most serious offenses were imaginative pranks—thousands of crickets turned loose in the high school classrooms, with teachers chasing the hopping critters while trying to look stern. A petty theft would provide everyone with a year's conversation about delinquency. Now, the halls and grounds have to be patrolled.

Two years ago, the faculty of this comparatively model high school were summoned to a meeting to discuss what was then a very recent deterioration of discipline. The principal admonished everyone on his failure to enforce the rules, especially the one requiring the removal of hats in all buildings. Many teachers shot back that such norms could not be enforced when they had no authority to punish transgressors. The principal, nevertheless, insisted that it was faculty responsibility to carry out his orders.

The morning after this meeting, Miss Hope reported for early (7:45 a.m.) duty in an isolated area. Among her tasks was to clear the locker area of students who had congregated there before the appointed time. They knew the rules, but every day a certain group of students defied them. One such habitual scofflaw was wearing a bright red cap on his head. "While you close your locker," Miss Hope said, "please also take off your hat." Without answering, he laughed and continued to fumble with his books. Sensing a good show, his cronies began to gather. Jeering, they said to him, "You ain't going to let that woman tell you what to do, are ya?" and to Miss Hope, "Whatcha wanta pick on him for?" Ignoring the gallery, Miss Hope asked the boy a second time to take off his hat and close the locker; and again he refused, amid much loud encouragement from his pack and a number of snide remarks. Miss Hope then told the boy to report to the office—at which he pushed her aside and walked away with his friends into an empty classroom, trailing over his shoulder, "Ain't nobody gonna tell me what to do."

Well, what option did Miss Hope have? She followed them into the room and ordered the offender a second time to report to the office. More students were gathering. The hooting and laughter and the threats grew louder. There was no way to contact help. She couldn't run. Several students, led by their ringleader in the red cap, brushed by her once more and escaped to the boys' rest room, across the hall, closeting themselves in. This gave Miss Hope an opportunity. She jammed her foot against the door and held them inside, hoping for some friendly face to appear before they threw their combined strength against her. A student finally did arrive on the scene, took in what was happening, and quietly slipped away to seek help. None arrived, however, before the gang forced their way out of the rest room. Miss Hope grabbed the arm of the boy who started it all. With his pack once again gathering around him, he stared down at her and said, "Take your hand off my permanent press."

Miss Hope saw red, then. She exploded with words that never in twenty years of professional teaching had she dreamed she would permit herself with students. "No, I will not take my hands off your permanent press," she said with deadly calm, "but if you move or say another word, as God is my witness, I shall see that you are permanently pressed in your coffin!"

There was absolute silence in the hall. He stood perfectly still. All she could feel was shock at her outburst. What had she been reduced to? The principal arrived at that moment and the students were taken to the office to give their side of the story.

Such troublemakers are never to blame and their excuses are standard: "I didn't understand what she said." "Who is she to tell me what to do?" "I didn't do nuttin." "People are always picking on me." The ringleader received a light admonition, the others were let go. A few hours later, Miss Hope returned to her hall for lunch period duty. She was still shaking from the events of the morning. An assistant principal, taking pity, offered to relieve her. She, of course, could not accept. To have been put to rout would have been a further weakening of not only her own but all teachers' authority. She couldn't claim she wasn't angry, or near tears, or bitterly wondering if she shouldn't resign. She couldn't say she wasn't scared, either, as she had reason to be. But it was a different fear—not of vengeance from the culprits, but of her own raging reaction to violence, which came from having been subjected to doses of deplorable behavior, humiliation and physical danger day after day.

During that interminable hour when she fought for her self-respect, a large rock was thrown at her. It came whizzing at her head from either a corner of the hall or a classroom. Fortunately, she saw it in time to duck.

These are the *quotidian* events in our schools. These

are simply a few of thousands of similar episodes that occur every day of the week in public institutions of education throughout the country. All of these disgusting scenes happened in Average Town, U.S.A., and those who were guilty were repeaters, every one. This is the atmosphere in which it is expected that education of the young will be accomplished; yet where one of these incidents took place, an administrator had the gall to boast publicly of his fiefdom that there were no disciplinary problems. Of course not, though teachers in that exemplary fiefdom are also required to patrol the hallways and grounds.

What has happened? Why has discipline broken down so utterly?

The first, and most obvious, cause is the change in the size and makeup of the population of our schools. The trend to consolidation of smaller facilities was based on sound economic and educational theory. A single, larger school could obviously operate less expensively than three smaller ones, and, at the same time, because of the increased number of students and faculty, offer a greater variety of courses and activities. What this city manager's approach did not take into account, however, was the corresponding loss in the amount of individual attention each student could receive and the severing of the close-knit relationship between the student and his alma mater and between the school and its neighborhood or community. Amalgamation took place at the sacrifice of these stabilizing values. Also, when a student body exceeds 800 or so, the individual becomes anonymous and can hide himself and his mischief in the crowd. Teachers and administrators, not being familiar with every face and name, are unable to identify offenders. Knowing this, unruly students defy authority at will, running away when confronted. The change in emphasis from a homely schoolhouse to a mass-production educational plant has been a mistake, because children are not products; they are human beings.

The battle for long-overdue equality under the law made matters worse. Brown vs. Board of Education, 1954, decreed that segregation of students into separate facilities based on race was in violation of the guarantees of the Fourteenth and Fifteenth Amendments. We welcomed Brown's thrust at the time, despite objections to the decision on procedural and even constitutional grounds, which do not concern us, and we still approve of its pioneering blow against discrimination of all kinds, leading as it did to the broader civil rights revolution that restored dignity to all our people. We do, however, take issue with the haste and manner in which many schools were integrated. The first plan was called Freedom of Choice: transfer from an all-black school to an all-white school was to be at the election of the individual student or his parents. This would have gradually altered a way of life that had obtained for ten generations. It would have allowed both races to adjust to an entirely different educational atmosphere and get used to each others' cultural idiosyncracies without the animosity that automatically arises when people are forced into radical change massively and all at once. There were, besides, organizational advantages. Freedom of choice would have permitted inter-racial cooperation in deciding what schools were to be closed down, which needed to be enlarged, where to move equipment from closed facilities, and how to make assignments for displaced faculty and administrators. Many communities, such as Camden, set up biracial committees to bring about a smooth and productive integration of their school systems, working together with the best of good-will.

Unfortunately, this gradualist approach was abandoned almost as soon as it got started. Zealous crusaders, to whom immediate integration of schools had become a single issue that obscured all other considerations, lobbied for draconian action. The fears of blacks as well as whites were disregarded. The redneck South was not to be allowed to obstruct social justice a single moment more. HEW demanded wholesale transfers of black students into formerly all-white institutions, and if there was not instant compliance, the government threatened loss of federal aid, while justices threatened to gavel school systems in contempt.

Schools were informed that they were, henceforth, to be color blind in regards to race . . . the usual contradiction following in the form of copious questionnaires that, among other things, required listing students in two columns, black and white. The federal government was anything but color blind. Overnight, moreover, it had swept aside the Tenth Amendment and in pursuit of higher morality *took control* of public education.

Many blacks had mixed feelings about the rush. Their children were going to receive a better education that would open opportunity for them, which was wonderful. On the other hand, it was certainly bruising to their children's pride to be designated as implicitly inferior because they had been taught in all-black institutions by all-black faculties. And many young people of both races resented being ordered by

executive or court order into a Utopia that they
neither recognized as such nor had had any part in
choosing. Common sense was trampled as ambitious
and, yes, also, well-meaning leaders of the nation gal-
loped roughshod over the deeply conservative feelings
of the young. Black students found themselves segregated academically within the integrated schools,
thus cruelly pointing out the deficiencies in their previous schooling. To remove this stigma, homogeneous
grouping, i.e. tracking (Chapter 11), was declared un-
constitutional, and administrators had to re-organize
classes to fit some social scientist's test-tube suspension of pigments without regard to ability or achievement. Black students were compelled to compete on a
one-to-one basis with whites, who, on the whole, were
in fact academically more advanced. The black students, therefore, felt even worse off. Their reaction,
naturally, was to withdraw, with the attitude that they
did not care. Though they could excel on the basketball
court or football field, most were unable to do so in the
classroom for cultural and other reasons. Since personal worth, as we said in Chapter XIII, tends to be
assessed in terms of academic averages alone—a de-
spicable intellectual snobbery—black children from
semi-literate urban and rural backgrounds felt
stripped of consequence. Their dignity as human beings, in the new situation, suffered even more grievous
assault. It is little wonder that chips grew on their
shoulders—that they reacted with bitterness and resorted to violence as one way of asserting their person-
hood. The Black Pantherism of the late 1960s was an
adult expression of the same syndrome.

We are not proposing sociological excuses for the
child who is prone by natural character to criminal

behavior. We simply do not believe that there are more such black than white children by genetic or other ordination. We are not ignoring the *machismo* of black youths, their cultural inheritance from African ancestors as warriors (if, after six or seven or more generations of cultural deracination, any substantive case can be advanced for such an inheritance); but ethnic *machismo,* in the first place, imagined or real, cannot be invoked to justify willful, intemperate, insubordinate, aggressive, violent, or criminal behavior in our society. Secondly, such rationalization of anti-social behavior runs into difficulties; all-black schools of the 1950s and before did not suffer in any statistically significant degree, that we are aware of, from the chronic violence that afflicts our *integrated* schools. Other reasons have to be sought to explain the difference.

We believe that difference lies in the accurate black perception that under the new circumstances, *because of a false hierarchy of values held by whites* and imposed on blacks by the predominantly white society, to which, in effect, blacks were being asked to *surrender,* their essential dignity in subtlest fashion was being disparaged. They rose up against this, instinctively, and with the only means of defense, as they saw it, at hand. And as some young blacks began adopting confrontation as a strategy—and because these earliest incidents were treated with kid gloves—the attitude fast spread among their friends that bad manners, rudeness, and even theft and assaults were the way to get attention. At about this time, many educators began asking, "If integration is a means of rescuing blacks from inferior instruction, why do the courts and HEW demand that these same presumably unfit

educators be appointed to the integrated institutions?"
The unfair consequence was to stigmatize *all* black
teachers and administrators as incompetent or unqualified. As a result, whites resented taking orders
from the blacks who were put over them as much as
black students resented taking orders from whites.

Government busybodiness further intensified the
backlash of these very human reactions. Although
schools were integrated in order to equalize opportunity for everybody, they were not allowed to operate on
this basis. As soon as administrators established a
program to comply with HEW's orders, they received
new directives. The black student quickly realized
that he was the focus of national attention and that he
was getting notice he had never dreamed of. He liked it
and wanted more. Who wouldn't? The concern for
equal and quality education was lost in the clamor
over the ratio of black cheerleaders, school representa-
tives, and athletes. Blacks began demanding "black
studies," black counselors, black administrators, and
more black teachers. The more they demanded, the
more they got, and the more resentful grew white
students. When a black student was punished for bad
behavior, he could, and frequently still does, cry "Discrimination." In many instances, administrators are
threatened with suits that can take years off anyone's
life, empty bank accounts, and almost certainly end in
a negative verdict and a ruined career. If more blacks
than whites are suspended, the principal is obliged to
prove that he is not being discriminatory. To state
bluntly that more black than white children get into
trouble is held to be irrelevant. In order to keep the
threatening power of HEW off their backs, administrators must be sure that the quota of black and white

students who are called on the carpet is in line with the ratio of black and white enrollment.

And, at a time when schools desperately need strong leadership, the powers that rule education, from the federal level down to local school boards, are at a comfortable distance from the realities of the institutions they control. Few, if any, have first-hand knowledge of what schools are really like today. These officials will tell you how they visit the schools to keep "in touch." Being a guest is one thing—being a worker in the vineyard is quite another. Sgt. Thor E. Bevins, a community-service officer in the Washington, D.C. police department, had this to say about the capital's educational establishment: "I dare any member of the school board to come in and try to run one of these schools. They wouldn't last until the water started boiling . . ."[2] Plato observed a good, long time ago that if men who made laws had to live by and under their laws there would be fewer and better laws. That's as true today as it was then.

In one community, the teachers and their principal appealed to the school board for help. The board was most solicitous. Government money was obtained to finance a meeting with a group of university professors (who willingly left their offices for a generous stipend) to advise them on their disciplinary problems. The only results were an official report that was presented to the board without the teachers or principal ever being informed what pearls of wisdom it might contain (close up the school?), and an article in the local newspaper about the wonderful results of the meeting. The discipline in that school has continued to deteriorate.

Veteran administrators and teachers who have first-hand knowledge of the school climate have also contributed to the demoralization of our public education. Even when dismayed by what they see and hear, they are no longer shocked, much less surprised. They have learned to submit in silence to blatant impudence for which a few years ago they would have demanded immediate expulsion. But, then, today, expulsion is the cardinal sin. All offenses—cutting class, forging an excuse, open defiance of authority, whatever—carry basically the same penalty regardless of the student's previous record. One official reaction to the growing public pressure to keep students in the classroom was dubbed "in-school suspension." The plan purported to get the delinquent child off the streets, to encourage him to mend his ways, to let him know that his disruptive behavior would not earn him a brief vacation through "out-of-school" suspension, and to allow him to continue his academic studies. The theory was seductive, and it did accomplish three of its goals, but the one that it did not achieve—improving conduct (the same names appeared over and over again on the list of suspensions)—is the one that affects the entire student body. A student who, by his disregard of the rules, deprives other students of *their* right to learn, should not be guaranteed what he has denied others. Simple equity demands this. He must be made to suffer the consequences of his selfishness. And when he knows there is a penalty to pay for misbehavior, he will think a long time before he penalizes himself.

There is no alternative. *A student who is guilty of continuous delinquency should be expelled.* He should be allowed neither to work his "suspension" off nor receive a few days vacation as a tap on the wrist. Nor should the school have to be his keeper or jailer.

Young and old view any plan in the light of its effect

upon them. Many programs established in public schools to aid the needy all too often backfire. The Free Lunch Program, for instance, was designed to assure deprived children of proper nutrition that is necessary for mental alertness as well as a healthy body; however, this project, as do many others, lost its effectiveness in its implementation. Deserving or not, the recipients are resented by fellow students who openly express their anger at what most of them perceive as a hand-out at their parents' expense and at their own in the near future. The free lunch children are thought of as freeloaders. This is especially the case when the tickets are so easily obtained. Application forms are made available to all students. An adult member of a family is required to furnish information about number of children, income, and hardships, and then sign the form. Approximately thirty to forty percent of a school population will present applications. These are "processed," which means that the child gets his free lunch unless someone questions his right to receive it. The National School Lunch Program, which administers this project through the State Department of Education ("and must comply with all requirements imposed by or pursuant to the Civil Rights Act of 1964 and the USDA Regulations"), requires a rather lengthy procedure to prove a child is not qualified. Also, trencher-children at the public board are carefully protected—they may not be pointed out *in any way.* No special lines, no differently colored coupons, and, goodness, gracious, no singing of any kind for their supper. If by chance they are identified, the administrator can find himself in the hottest government water. But despite this careful camouflage, students know who is and who is not eating at public expense. Many young people brag about their "free" tickets and openly flaunt cleverness by flipping their "spending money" in the faces of schoolmates.

This program has taught many young people and adults to defraud the American taxpayer. The damage it has done far outweighs its contributions. A student in high school can and should be expected to earn his lunch by doing odd jobs such as serving food, cleaning tables, and washing chalk boards. This would protect him from the resentment of his fellows. There is nothing degrading in working for one's daily bread. (Far from it, not long ago this was standard practice.) Children regularly earn their allowances at home by doing simple chores. The student who in the same manner earns his lunch ticket has nothing to be ashamed of, and assuring good hot food for the poor in this manner would obviate the need for expensive federal bureaus of administration.

We could beat the subject to death. Government must retreat from its unwarranted interference in education. Politicians do not know what they are doing. They have no knowledge of the field and only the most superficial exposure to its complexities. The best-intentioned philanthropic programs, such as the two we've mentioned here, are pernicious ethically and morally, promoting discord, dependency, and an attitude of care-free hedonism that prepares children in the poorest manner for adulthood. There are, as well, too many strings attached to every government initiative, overloading administrative staffs in our high and grammar schools; and the ideological absolutism that imposes a mathematical quota taken to three digits across the decimal point on everything from the distribution of academic laurels to the supposedly even-handed meeting of discipline is as silly as it is obnoxious, disfiguring elementary justice for the sake of an unachievable perfect equality, and meanwhile transforming our schools into bull pits where antagonism between the races grows instead of diminishing. It does not help, either, when misguided judges keep dumping problem children into schools instead of into the correctional institutions where they belong. Our schools cannot be reformatories; teachers and administrators are not wardens. It is totally unfair to penalize—in some cases, terrorize—the well-behaved children of both races who want to learn, by placing in their midst hoodlums whose sole intention is to disrupt the educational process in as many ways as they are able.

Heavily accountable though they are, however, misguided juvenile courts, ideological zealots, and bureaucrats are not alone to blame. Parents and educators must also demand civilized behavior. We, the public, have been supine on two counts: in disciplining our own children and in resisting the encroachments on local schooling by the educational establishment. We must wrest back from politicians authority over *our* young. We must reject the envious Rousseauian concept that children are creatures of the state and that the sole end of their education is to make them better servitors. It is not for some department in Washington or a double plus ungood Orwellian Ministry of Thought Control to set educational and sociological values, which tomorrow may be as wrong or corrupt as we presume them to be benign today, and mold our children into unquestioning ideological clones. This is not Russia. This is not China. We must free our children from the ever-increasing claims of Leviathan;

and in this battle for emancipation professional educational associations must ally themselves with an aroused public instead of currying the favor of Washington, as too often they do today, becoming a political lobby whose interests are identical with that of the empire builders—self-serving instead of serving.

This having been accomplished—we, the public, having regained authority over the cultural and academic rearing of our children—we must ourselves show more spine than many of us, as parents, have wanted to, even though it may happen that the consequences fall on one of our own offspring. Were we adults so poorly treated as minors that we feel compelled to shield our children from similar experiences? Conversely, were we so leniently reared that we feel guilty imposing rules of conduct that we ourselves were not required to observe? Whatever the reason, we have given our young the keys of the car while refusing the driving lessons, hiding the handbook of traffic regulations, and blindfolding the patrolman. What do we do now—pray for a miracle as we wait for the crash?

Surely not! Mistakes can be corrected. The educational climate can be changed. Much that is mischievous in the public schools can be eradicated by reversing directions in those cases where methods and programs have created trouble. To insist on freedom and rights for one child through means that deny many other children theirs is neither wise, nor fair, nor democratic. To give free rein to *all* young people before they are mature is not kind, not sensible, and the most mistaken of love. Punishment for infraction of rules must be swift, sure, and truly blind in terms of justice. Parents in their turn must support educators in these painful matters, helping the schools return to what

just twenty years ago were accepted as normal standards of civility.

Well, we haven't mentioned the Ramseur System,
have we? That's by way of confessing that only a major
reversal of sociological perceptions can deal definitely
with the bedlam that passes for public education. But
while we wait for that reversal to take place, there *is* a
single, practical step that can be taken whose effectiveness as an aid to the restoration of order can be
astonishing. It should be adopted at once, and on a
massive scale.

We realize that there are still neighborhoods where
children from similar (and usually comfortable) backgrounds walk to school every day in safety and pursue
their education in a peaceful setting. Their parents
may arch eyebrows over what they consider to be our
exaggerated concern. Such people—who are indeed
extraordinarily privileged to be insulated from one of
the major concerns of ordinary folk—cluck their
tongues over the intolerance of the provincial masses
and pass off school violence as a necessary evil of the
brave new world. Most of us aren't so sanguine. We
want no part of a society where ordinary people are
threatened as a matter of course in property and in
their very lives. Disregard for civility has to be nipped
in the bud, and right now; and the technological mar-
vel that will do this is the mechanical eye, closed
circuit television.

One afternoon, a year or so ago, workmen installed a
light on a tall pole atop the gymnasium of our school.
The rumor ran through the student body that it was a
camera. You wouldn't believe the effect. For three
whole days—until everybody learned that it was just a
night light—peace reigned. Kids aren't dumb. They

reckoned that if one camera had been placed, there
would be others. No chances were taken. What a delightful interlude those three days were! So delightful
in fact, that several teachers began investigating the
operation, uses, and cost of closed circuit television.

We served on that committee. Among the questions
we asked ourselves were: How does the system operate? What are the objections to using it? How will
television detect or prevent crime, or both? The answers we came up with, we believe, should persuade
school boards everywhere to consider this protective
measure seriously.

The system covers all grounds, hallways, and stair-
wells. All traffic is viewed on television screens that
are concentrated in one room. Instead of standing
about like so many targets, teachers can monitor the
screens under the same schedule they follow now. The
only difference is that they can see a great deal more,
can actually get to enjoy their lunch period (which
they often have to skip when they are picketed in
corridors and playgrounds), and can tape incidents for
the permanent record by merely pushing a button. The
film supplies concrete proof of what is going on. It can
be used again and again, and can be erased for a
re-run, recording a new day. The cameras are so placed
that anybody moving about the school passes from the
range of one into the range of another. We asked ourselves, "But couldn't someone shatter a lens?" Sure,
but whoever tries it will star on the film that convicts
him. He is taped as he stalks his objective, and his
vandalism will not escape the purview of other
cameras. (His only hope is to be a dead-eye shot with a
sling or air gun at a considerable distance.) As we say,
kids aren't dumb: no one is likely to be so foolish as to

trap himself in such a way. To make sure that they get the point, students should be advised just how the surveillance system works, why it is there, and how it will be used.

The principal objections we encountered in our study were the expense and the prison-like atmosphere that such invigilation would allegedly produce. If that's the case, many supermarkets, banks, apartment houses, museums, and department stores are prison-like; increasingly, they use closed circuit television, harried as they are by the shoplifting and vandalism that bedevil our society and that, as we contend, often got their start by going uncorrected in public schools. We would counter, besides, that the aura of menace that prevades so many of our schools has of itself already created a prison atmosphere, with law-abiding students and their teachers the victims.

As for expense, let's consider. In 1974, the cost of crime and violence in schools ran to $600 million nationwide, and that figure continues to climb. New York City educators should scoff at expense. There, it's been calculated, the cost of replacing broken windows for a single year would pay for six new educational plants. Our school consists of six separate buildings that sit on three acres, with a capacity of 1600 students. The committee that investigated closed circuit television got an estimate of $28,000 for a system that provided complete protection. The board refused to go along, deeming it too costly. That same board, however, at the next meeting, approved an expenditure of approximately $44,000 to increase the size of the football stadium for the principal benefit of approximately thirty boys and their fans. It seems to depend on what the priorities are, doesn't it?

A great blessing of closed circuit television is that the cameras are sleepless. They keep on running and recording whatever goes on during the hours when school personnel aren't available or the buildings and grounds are shut. Since no lock was ever devised that a determined adolescent can't pick or break, only an unimpeachable witness to such acts can discourage them. The camera's eye is such, unblinking, constant, and merciless. Teachers will welcome it. During the day, acts of insolence or insubordination, in all their crudity, are taped and provide the necessary evidence for swift retribution. Is this unfair? Then think of the children. How would you like it if you were a twelve year old girl budding into pubescence and someone brushed against you, ran his hands over you, and made obscene remarks? How would you like to live in daily dread of going to school? The camera's frigid eye will freeze evidence of any sort of harassment.

The benefits are so numerous that the mention of just a few more ought to suffice. Students who "float," as we say, through the halls during class periods looking for something to destroy or someone to frighten are quickly identified. Drug pushers can't escape the ever vigilant sweep of the lens. There are teachers who seem to have as much trouble staying in a classroom as students. They are caught out, helping the principal maintain staff discipline.

We've spoken of how forced, instant and massive integration, poorly planned and bureaucratically boshed, has divided the children of the two races into hostile camps instead of drawing them together. They are formally integrated in the classrooms; they get along on athletic teams and fraternize to a degree in other student activities; but there is scant socializing under unstructured conditions, and antagonism lies just below the surface, heated by the embers of deep mutual suspicion. Blacks believe that they receive more punishment than whites, that they are picked on, and whites are convinced of the contrary: that blacks are guilty of most of the disturbances and get off scot free. One side calls up witnesses; the other side calls up witnesses. Most investigations depend on one person's say-so, or hearsay, and sometimes even the victim of a beating or rape can't summon the necessary testimony to convict. The unbiased camera can be the answer. It simply shows what happened. Knowing that they are thus protected, and that their mechanical supervisor records only the truth, students can go about the business of acquiring an education and mixing with their friends without fear of intimidation from anyone on school grounds. Once peace and quiet descend upon their world, they can open their eyes, look around them, and maybe even get to know each other, relieved as they are of the barriers of fear ond hostility. They may, on their own (*mirabile dictu*), without outside exhortation, moralizations, or injunctions, decide that they like each other. It would be more than sufficient if they came to respect each other's human worth, which, freed of cant as well as fear and hostility, could come about.

If parents and school officials had been more conscious of the changing climate of public education, they could have prevented the misbegotten programs and counterproductive permissiveness that, together, have turned our schools into concentration camps. What wrongheaded policies have been imposed on our schools in the holy names of progress, behavioral determinism, and a host of other half-baked sociological revelations, and how our poor children have suffered from them! We in the first instance level our criticism at those officials who incubate their grand designs in private offices and lay the law down via typed directives. We include visiting professors and consultants, most of them sponsored by state or federal grants, who patronizingly advise educators in the field how to do what they themselves have never once in their lives personally attempted and what, in the intimacy of their souls, they pray they are never called upon to attempt. These are the sultans and nabobs of public education. They control it and direct it. Their titles are as various as the leaves of springtime: Secretary of Education, Superintendent, Assistant Superintendent, Member of the Whatzit's? Board, Director of Something, Coordinator of Anything, Advisor to All. Regardless of title, their limitation is that *those who make the rules do not play the game.* They're not even called upon to watch the game! Cameras can do that for them.

Parents, saddest to tell, are similarly ignorant of what goes on in the contemporary public school. They don't dream, for example, of the transformation that can come over their angelic daughters when they leave home and enter the premises of PHS # 12, whether in personality or even dress. We're reminded of a teacher, a friend, who recently investigated laughter from the off-limits faculty rest rooms. There she found three girls happily changing from neat, attractive clothes to sexually provoking attire. Parents do not know the 8:00 a.m. to 3:00 p.m. world that their children inhabit and can be changed by. If they're interested, however—and we think they are—that world can be visited for them through the mechanical eye of closed circuit television, dispelling their innocence. The camera, in our opinion, is vital. Dare we say it?—more vital than the band, cheerleaders, and enlarged gladiatorial arenas.

The Ramseur System can resolve the academic crisis of public education. It is doing so in the school system where, for the past fifteen years, it has been put into practice. The Ramseur System, within the classroom, as we have shown, alleviates all those social or structural problems normally to be expected in a school, by its nature promoting an environment of disciplined purpose. But where incorrigibles are concerned, until every other substantive reform that we've proposed is adopted, only the camera will help.

Footnotes, Chapter XIV

[1] Franke, David and Holly Franke, *Safe Places; East of the Mississippi,* Arlington House, 1972, Paperback Library, 1973.

[2] "Terror In Schools," *U.S. News & World Report,* January 6, 1976, p. 55.

[3] Title of Education Amendment of 1972. Federal Legislation.

Chapter XV
Here Is Tomorrow

We conceived the Ramseur System to lay the foundation for a promising tomorrow. What it does, above all, is to respect the child—this is the essence of it—by thrusting on him responsibility for his successes and failures, thus not only building into his character *self*-respect but teaching him to earn now what he will need for his future. The design is consistent with the character that is required of a people who govern themselves. Govern them*selves*. Self-discipline as a general practice is unpopular today. Frugality has almost disappeared from the rhetoric of our times. The fruits of skill and labor are deprecated, and people speak slurringly of a "meritocracy"; but as Ben Franklin remarked with mordant pertinence when he was asked what the upshot was in Philadelphia, "Well, you've got a republic, if you can keep it."[1]

Popular government, our right to govern ourselves, never came cheaply. We not only had to wrest our freedom from the British in the past; we have had to earn it and work hard to keep it from generation to generation. We are at this moment deeply disturbed by threats to that freedom not only without but within from a government that, it is generally agreed, has grown too powerful and intrusive. Another way of putting it is that our government has ceased to respect its citizens. Daniel Webster has warned us:

Good intentions will always be pleaded for every assumption of power. . . . It is hardly too strong to say that the Constitution was made to guard the people against the dangers of good intentions. There are men in all ages who mean to govern well, but they mean to govern. They promise to be good masters, but they mean to be masters.

The nationwide tax rebellion that began in California in the spring of 1978 and many other popular rebuffs since of the omnipotent complex in Washington show that, as a people, we have come to recognize this. It is no longer an ideological or class perception. Democrats and Republicans, "liberals" and "conservatives," laborers and white collar workers, farmers and manufacturers, blacks and whites all, in different degree and for sometimes contrary reasons, more and more distrust the bureaucratic state that year after year arrogates to itself those powers and areas of sovereign choice that under our Constitution were supposed to reside in the people and that spell the difference between a free and an authoritarian society. What we have not yet come to recognize is the logical corollary, or connection, between authoritarian government and a populace that has grown soft, self-indulgent, slothful, uncertain of its abilities, muddled in its powers to think, ethically confused, profligate, and abandoned to the pursuit of sensual and material pleasures (the pursuit of happiness is a different thing), and thus increasingly dependent on an ever-expanding central government and its services. But what we have to fight is not only such as those benighted politicians in our country who would, today, despite growing opposition, concentrate even greater power in Washington: it is ourselves; our hedonism, our ethical turpitude, our longing for the Free Lunch, our abandonment of the values that alone gave hope to this experiment in self-government. We have to regain *our* self-respect. We have to regain it by earning it in our own minds.

De Gaulle said it, cynical statesmen in all ages have thought it: "People get the government they deserve." If we want to retain—some say recover—our republic, we need to exercise self-discipline and reapprentice ourselves to the wisdom that comes from holding expectations to bounds and distinguishing realities from illusions. For a free society to survive, an intellectually and morally rigorous citizenry, as well as a compassionate citizenry (compassion consisting in the imaginative projection of oneself into another's condition, and therefore an act of the sensitive intellect—not gushing sentiment, which is essentially a form of narcissism), are essential. Since the Ramseur System offers no illusions of grandeur, learning under RPL is learning how to live up to the demanding human standards of a democratic system, whose premise must be that the individual citizen is a responsible being, with all the risk that this dignity implies.

Under the guise of love, children have been granted diplomas with a mere stroke of the pen; they have been allowed, even encouraged, to make policies and decisions about their future before they have learned about living in the present. They have been denied the challenge and joy of youth. What are their dreams for tomorrow? They will have to be more of the same. What do they do when they discover, in the future, that the games they play do have a price and the player must put up his ante? Who will lift their burdens and bear their pain when they fail or someone fails them? Will they know how to change their direction or what direction to take? They most certainly have not been trained for this; and until they are, they can never achieve professional or personal fulfillment. Handicapped as they now are in its pursuit, happiness will elude them like a will-o'-the-wisp, because they have no notion in what true happiness consists. Will they run from every challenge, relying on their "rights," until they are incapacitated to engage and overcome any obstacle whatever; and all because they have been denied the most important of human rights—that of shouldering the responsibility for oneself with courage and confidence and freely discharging one's obligations to society?

Children today have been flattered, pampered, and pacified. In the name of love—which can be a cover for not wanting to be bothered—children have been given without being asked to give in turn. In all things they are excused. If they do not behave, their delinquency is the fault of their parents; if they do not learn, their ignorance is the fault of educators; if they do not obey the laws, their lawlessness is the fault of the system; if they are apathetic, their boredom is the fault of society. And all their problems are charged to youth, which makes them *ipso facto* blameless. So these blameless apprentice hedonists are allowed to behave as they choose, learn only what pleases them, abide by the rules that suit them, and bear none of the consequences for their choices. They are even allowed to remain anonymous—until life catches up with them.

Which of us would sacrifice our tomorrow in return for all today? Tomorrow is our reward. The promise of tomorrow is the motivation for our actions this day and the next. Man's need to be a part of the future, even beyond his life's span, is vital to the strength and

growth of nations. His contributions to the future are
the legacy he leaves to his children.

What is it that we want for our young—freedom,
through ignorance and indulgence, to repeat every
error that we and past generations have made, or
inculation in the wisdom that mankind has acquired
from the long history of past blunders so that the next
generation may hope to avoid repeating at least some
of them? Myth it may be, but mankind's capacity to
learn truth is the premise of the free society. "Freedom," wrote in his secret diary the doomed and
wretched Winston Smith of George Orwell's *1984,* "is
the freedom to say that two plus two make four. If that
is granted, all else follows." We are not teaching our
children to add two plus two in school; we are not
teaching them to add up the realities in life, to seek the
true cause of the unpleasant effect. We are fettering
them, morally and intellectually, instead of endowing
them with the ability to recognize their mistakes early
so that they may profit from them while there is still
life enough left to turn around in, the social conscience
to embrace their obligations to others so that they may
know the security and love found in shared humanity,
the humility and fortitude to accept disappointments
and make of them a spur for continued effort, and the
temperance to space their lives so that each moment
can be lived to its fullest and so that idleness becomes a
restorative interlude instead of occasion for despair.
Perhaps most important, we should be training them
in the judgement to discriminate between love and
self-righteousness, and, in general, what is good or
meritorious from what is meretricious.

All these virtues we can implant in our children if
we spend less time searching for their approval and

more time *really* loving them. Let us prove that by denying them those things that we know they are too young to handle and others that we know they will profit from more in the future than now; by giving them direction and purpose in play and work; by giving them the best, not always the most entertaining, education; by disciplining them so that they may learn to discipline themselves.

Maybe this mother said it better than we can. Elizabeth, her daughter, was not the easiest child to raise; spankings were all too often a daily ritual. One day, when Elizabeth had been punished for still another peccadillo, she hurled at her mother, "You don't love me." Her mother knelt and said, "Oh, yes, I do. You may be too young to understand, but let me tell you how much I love you. I shall do whatever is needed to make you the kind of person whom others will love and protect when I am no longer here."

What can begin only in the home must be confirmed in the schoolhouse.

Footnote, Chapter XV

[1] Max Farrand, *The Fathers of the Constitution,* Yale University Press, 1921, pp. 134–135.